FENG SHUI

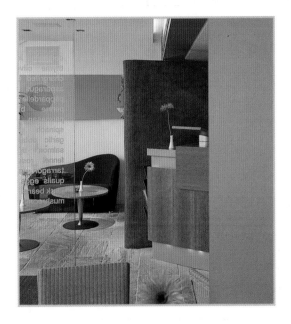

FOR A SUCCESSFUL OFFICE

HOW TO CREATE A HARMONIOUS WORKING ENVIRONMENT

GILL HALE

southwater

This edition is published by Southwater

Southwater is an imprint of
Anness Publishing Limited
Hermes House
88-89 Blackfriars Road
London SE1 8HA
tel. 020 7401 2077
fax 020 7633 9499

Distributed in the UK by
The Manning Partnership
251-253 London Road East
Batheaston
Bath BA1 7RL
tel. 01225 852 727
fax 01225 852 852

Distributed in the USA by
Anness Publishing Inc.
27 West 20th Street
Suite 504, New York
NY 10011
tel. 212 807 6739
fax 212 807 6813

Distributed in Australia by
Sandstone Publishing
Unit 1, 360 Norton Street
Leichhardt
New South Wales 2040
tel. 02 9560 7888
fax 02 9560 7488

1 3 5 7 9 10 8 6 4 2

Publisher: Joanna Lorenz
Project Editor: Helen Marsh
Designer: Nigel Partridge
Special Photography: John Freeman
Stylist: Claire Hunt
Illustrator: Geoff Ball
Production Controller: Don Campaniello

Previously published as part of a larger compendium, *The Practical Encyclopedia of Feng Shui*

CONTENTS

INTRODUCTION

Feng Shui is basically an environmental science and its origins are simple. It is based on an interpretation of the natural world which enabled the Chinese to create efficient agricultural systems, and also the study of the movement of heavenly bodies in order to determine the passage of time. Over the centuries, the interpretation grew more complex and became removed from its original purpose. Fortunately the ancient Chinese preserved the information in written form. In essence, all societies still retain the knowledge contained in Feng Shui, but it has become

absorbed into different disciplines. By understanding the basic concepts and applying them to

the modern world we can choose designs, meaningful images and symbols from our own cultures to support us in our lives.

As practised today, Feng Shui gives us advice on how to create environments in which we feel comfortable and supported. Many of us spend much of our lives at work and our surroundings there are as important as in our homes. We usually have little control over the location or building we work in, but awareness of factors which can affect us will enable us to minimize problems. Interior decorations are also often beyond our control, but we may be able to influence them. We usually have some control over individual work spaces and can arrange these and our desks so that we feel comfortable as we work. By taking positive steps to improve our working environment, we can connect to the energy of the spaces around us and bring about desired changes to how we feel and to our performance.

The buildings we work in are part of a larger environment which can have a profound effect on our state of mind and on our wellbeing. The first impression a client has of an organization is crucial and we should endeavour to ensure that this is favourable.

Attention to detail at the entrance to a building and in the reception area will be amply rewarded and can inspire confidence in a company. Feng Shui can offer advice to businesses even before clients visit and the first impressions offered by business logos and stationery can substantially affect customer perception. Feng Shui attempts to create smooth energy flows, so communications channels are crucial and an efficient telephone system – often the first point of contact – is extremely important. Timing is often crucial to the success or failure of a move or a project and Feng Shui can offer advice on how to determine the best time to proceed.

Modern lifestyles leave us little time to stop and consider the effect our surroundings have on us. There is increasing awareness that some aspects of modern technology, the materials we use and the substances we release into the atmosphere can create lasting damage to our health and to the planet. Although this is not Feng Shui in its purest form, concern for our environment and an awareness of the damage we inflict on it must form part of Feng Shui for today. One effect of modern working conditions, Sick Building Syndrome, is now accepted as a problem and often when we feel under the weather, lighting, chemicals from machinery and materials and recirculated air can often be the cause.

Feng Shui also takes account of personalities, and interaction with work colleagues is often the prime cause of stress within a business. Realising the strengths, weaknesses and working

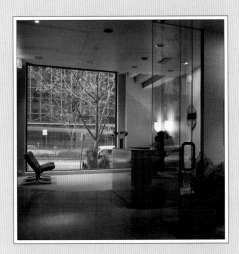

methods of those around us can help us to channel them and ourselves into positive situations, rather than struggling on in in a negative one. Self-knowledge can greatly assist us in our careers and this book offers us advice on how we can use the principles of Feng Shui in the office, at home, when travelling and in interviews to help us achieve our full potential. Feng Shui offers us the opportunity to achieve health, happiness and well-being through living in harmony with our environment and others within it.

WHAT IS FENG SHUI?

The Chinese have a saying, "First, luck; second, destiny; third, Feng Shui; fourth, virtues; fifth, education": although Feng Shui can be a powerful force in shaping our lives, it is not a cure for all ills. Luck plays a major role, and personality, or karma, is almost as important. What we do with our lives and how we behave towards others will play a part, and education gives us the tools to make sense of the world. Feng Shui is just one part of the complete package.

▲ *In China the dragon symbolizes good fortune. Its presence is felt in landforms and watercourses.*

The single factor which sets Feng Shui apart from other philosophical systems is that it has the capacity for change built into it. Most systems evolved from similar principles; understanding the natural world played a major role and natural phenomena were believed to be imbued with a spirit or deity, recognition of which would give people some benefit in their lives. Where these systems became established as religions, the deities were worshipped, but Feng Shui has remained a philosophy and can be used in any culture and alongside any belief system.

▲ *The Dragon Hills which protect Hong Kong are believed to be responsible for its prosperity.*

▶ *Much of the symbolic imagery in Feng Shui is taken from landscapes such as this in Guilin, southern China.*

Feng Shui uses formulae which determine the rising and falling energy in a given time span of an individual or a house. Other formulae indicate a person's best location within a home or office, and can suggest the best placing of beds and desks. Many Chinese people consult astrologers annually to further refine this, so that every activity within the year can be pinpointed accurately and undertaken at an auspicious time. This can be as pre-cise as the best time to conceive or even when to wash your hair.

The philosophy of Feng Shui is embraced by people who are aware of the impact their surroundings have on them and feel the need to take action to improve their lives, but using Feng Shui correctly is a skill and its principles can-not be adapted simply to suit the circumstances of a place or an individual.

▼ *Our surroundings affect us. Fresh air, natural products and a healthy environment enhance our mental and physical well-being.*

Feng Shui enables us to position our-selves within our environment to our best advantage. The positioning of our hous-es and offices as well as their internal design affects each of us positively or neg-atively. Feng Shui helps us to determine the most favourable positions for us and the layouts, colours and designs which will support us. In the garden we can determine the best locations for the dif-ferent activities we intend to pursue there, but we also have to take account of the plants in the garden and their needs, which are equally important if the environment is to thrive.

▲ *Water energy plays a significant role in Feng Shui. Here a fountain brings life to an office courtyard.*

The following chapters provide infor-mation on those aspects of this complex and fascinating subject that can be uti-lized by everyone in their own space. When we introduce Feng Shui into our lives we can only benefit, even where we only touch the surface. As we become more aware of our surroundings, and actively begin to change those factors with which we feel uncomfortable, we begin to gain a deeper insight into our-selves and our part in the wider picture.

▼ *The T'ung Shui almanac, produced for centuries, details the best times to move house, conceive and even wash your hair.*

APPROACHES TO FENG SHUI

Feng Shui is about interpreting environments. Practitioners use a number of different approaches to connect with the energy or "feel" of a place, and fine-tune it to make it work for those living or working there. Provided the principles are understood, the different approaches will be effective. More often than not, practitioners use a mixture of methods to create the effects they want.

THE ENVIRONMENTAL APPROACH

In ancient times, people lived by their wits and knowledge of local conditions. Their needs were basic: food and shelter. Observation would tell them from which direction the prevailing winds were coming and they would build their homes in protective sites. They needed water in order to grow and transport their crops so rivers were important, and the direction of the flow and the orientation of the banks would determine the type of crops which could be grown. This branch of Feng Shui is known as the Form or Landform School and was the earliest approach to the subject.

▲ *These "Karst" limestone hills in China symbolically protect an area of rich agricultural land.*

▼ *The Form School regards this as the ideal spot on which to build. The Black Tortoise hill at the rear offers support while the White Tiger and Green Dragon give protection from the wind, with the all-powerful dragon slightly higher than the Tiger. The Red Phoenix marks the front boundary, and the river irrigates the site and enables crops to be transported for trade.*

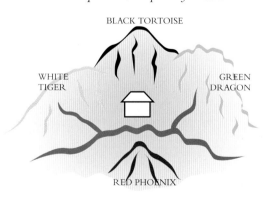

BLACK TORTOISE

WHITE TIGER

GREEN DRAGON

RED PHOENIX

▶ *A luo pan or compass, used by geomancers in ancient China. Much of the information it records is regularly used by Feng Shui consultants.*

THE COMPASS APPROACH

In ancient China, geomancers investigated earth formations and watercourses while astronomers charted the skies. Those who understood the power of the information they possessed recorded their knowledge on an instrument called a luo pan, or compass. The luo pan illustrates not only direction, but also investigates the energy of each direction, depending on the landform or heavenly body to be found there. Interpreting these energies suggests suitable sites for human beings. Feng Shui is based on the *I Ching*, a philosophical book which interprets the energies of the universe. Its 64 images from the yearly nature cycle form the outer ring of the luo pan. With the wisdom of ancient sages added to it over the centuries, the *I Ching* offers us a means to connect to the natural flow of the universe. Its built-in time factor allows individuals to connect to it in different ways at different times in their lives.

THE INTUITIVE APPROACH

Ancient texts illustrate every shape of mountain and watercourse. The names illustrate concepts significant to the Chinese psyche. "Tiger in Waiting" suggests a negative place, where residents will never be able to relax, whereas "Baby Dragon Looking at its Mother" indicates a much more restful environment.

The ancient text of the *Water Dragon Classic* provides more information on the best places to build, showing flow direction and position within the tributaries, with the names again indicating the type of environment. The sensibilities of people living and working on the land were finely tuned and their knowledge of the natural world endowed them with an instinct for suitable sites to grow crops.

▶ *Mountain sites (1 & 2) and river sites (3 & 4); the dots represent buildings. All except for "Tiger in Waiting" are auspicious positions to build a new home.*

▼ *This prime site is protected by mountains, with healthy watercourses.*

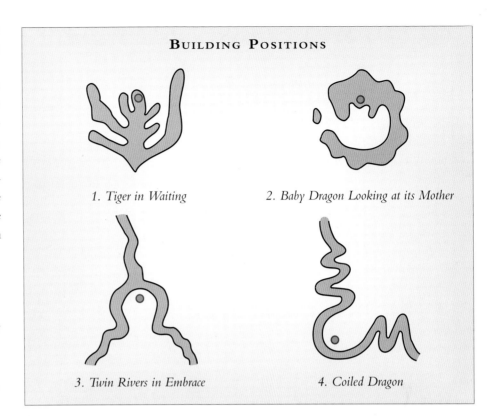

BUILDING POSITIONS

1. Tiger in Waiting

2. Baby Dragon Looking at its Mother

3. Twin Rivers in Embrace

4. Coiled Dragon

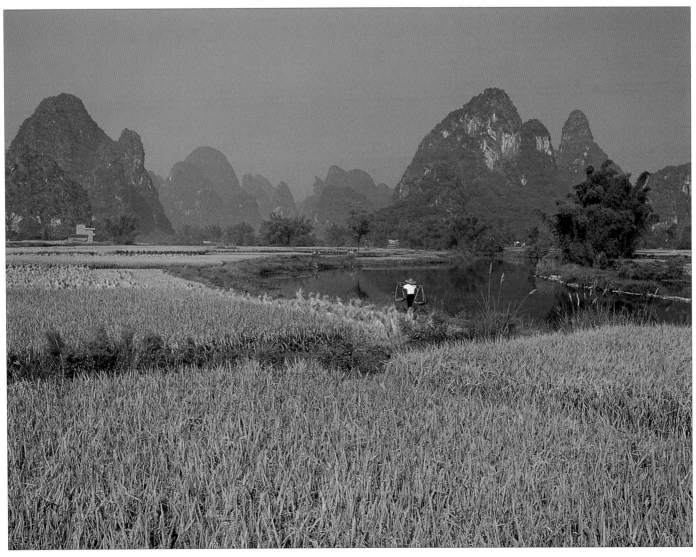

THE PRINCIPLES OF FENG SHUI

Ancient peoples regarded the heavens, the earth and themselves as part of one system. This holistic view of life persists in many cultures, where health and medicine, food and lifestyle, and the route to salvation are all interconnected in one ecological system.

THE WAY

The Tao, or the Way, the philosophy of which underlies Feng Shui, shows how to order our lives to live in harmony with ourselves, each other and the natural world. We can use Feng Shui to help us work towards achieving this.

▼ *"The Dragon Breathing on the Lake" – the lake is a powerful Chinese image, symbolizing a light-reflective surface harbouring a dark and deep interior.*

YIN AND YANG

Positive and negative forces act together in order to create energy – in electricity, for instance. Yin and yang represent these two forces which are in constant movement, each attempting to gain dominance. Where one achieves dominance, an imbalance occurs, so when one

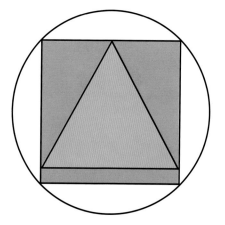

force becomes too strong its influence subsides and the other takes over. Still water, for example, is yin; a raging torrent is yang. Imagine a slow-moving yin river. When it hits rocks and descends, turbulence occurs, it speeds up and becomes yang. When it flows into a lake, it slows down and becomes yin once more. Yin and yang are opposing but interdependent concepts – without the idea of cold we would not be able to describe heat. At their extremes they

▲ *The T'ai Chi symbol illustrates the concept of yin and yang, the opposite yet interdependent forces that drive the world.*

◄ *Circle, Square, Triangle – signifying Heaven, Earth, human beings – the universal cosmological symbol.*

YIN	YANG
Moon	Sun
Winter	Summer
Dark	Light
Feminine	Masculine
Interior	Exterior
Low	High
Stillness	Movement
Passive	Active
Odd numbers	Even numbers
Earth	Heaven
Cold	Heat
Soft	Hard
Valleys	Hills
Still water	Mountains
Gardens	Houses
Sleep	Wakefulness

change into each other; ice can burn and sunstroke sufferers shiver. The aim is to achieve a balance between them. There are examples throughout the book of how we can achieve this in our own environments. Some of the more common associations are listed left.

CHI

Chi is a concept unknown in Western philosophy but figures repeatedly in the philosophies of the East. It is the life force of all animate things, the quality of environments, the power of the sun, the moon and weather systems, and the driving force in human beings. In China, the movements in T'ai Chi encourage chi to move through the body. Acupuncture needles are used to unblock its flow when stuck. Chinese herbal medicine uses the special energetic qualities of herbs to correct chi when it becomes unbalanced. Meditation helps to establish a healthy mind: every brush stroke of the Chinese artist or sweep of the calligrapher's pen is the result of trained mental processes and the correct breathing

▼ *An acupuncturist at work. The needles unblock the energy channels and enable chi to flow round the body.*

▲ *Chinese people practising T'ai Chi. The exercises are designed to aid the flow of chi in the body.*

techniques, which ensure that each carefully composed painting or document is infused with chi.

The purpose of Feng Shui is to create environments in which chi flows smoothly to achieve physical and mental health. Where chi flows gently through a house, the occupants will be positive and will have an easy passage through life. Where chi moves sluggishly or becomes stuck, then the chances are that problems will occur in the day-to-day life or long-term prospects of those living there.

Where chi flows smoothly in the garden, the plants will be healthy and the wildlife there will flourish. Animals, birds, insects and the myriad of unseen micro-organisms that live there will regulate themselves and create a balanced and supportive environment. Where chi cannot flow unimpeded and becomes sluggish or stuck, an area may become dank or there may be an imbalance which creates, say, a plague of aphids.

In an office where chi flows freely, employees will be happy and supportive, projects will be completed on time and stress levels will be low. Where the chi is stuck, there will be disharmony and the business will not flourish.

FIVE TYPES OF ENERGY

Some of the latest scientific theories enable us to make sense of the ancient formulae on which Feng Shui is based. It is accepted that everything in the universe vibrates. All our senses and everything we encounter are attuned to certain frequencies, which react with us in a positive or negative way. We are all familiar with sound waves, which bring us radio, and electromagnetic waves, which bring us television. Colours, shapes, food, weather conditions – everything in our lives affects us on a vibrational level for good or ill and, in turn, we react in various yet predictable ways, depending on our individual traits.

The concept of elements exists throughout the world. The Chinese recognize five which arise out of the interplay of yin and yang and represent different manifestations of chi. They represent a classification system for everything in the universe, including people, some of these are shown in the "Relationships of the Five Elements" table.

Ideally, there should be a balance of all the elements. Where one dominates or is lacking, then difficulties occur. Interpreting and balancing the elements plays a major part in the practice of Feng Shui. The elements move in a predetermined way, illustrated as a cycle in which they all support each other. A useful way of remembering this is by looking at the cycle in the following way. Water enables Wood to grow, Wood enables Fire to burn resulting in ashes or Earth, in which forms Metal, which in liquid

form resembles Water. Another cycle indicates how the elements control each other and can be memorized as follows: Water extinguishes Fire, and in turn is soaked up by the Earth, which is depleted of energy by Wood in the form of trees, which can be destroyed by Metal tools. the "Relationships of the Five Elements" table introduces another aspect – how in supporting another element, an element can itself be weakened. The applications of the five elements are illustrated throughout this book.

▲ *Storms are nature's way of restoring a balance. They replenish negative ions in the atmosphere, which improves air quality.*

▼ *The heavenly bodies are essential to our lives and their movements lie at the heart of Feng Shui.*

THE RELATIONSHIPS OF THE FIVE ELEMENTS

ELEMENT	HELPED BY	HARMED BY	WEAKENED BY	WEAKENS
Wood	Water	Metal	Fire	Earth
Fire	Wood	Water	Earth	Metal
Earth	Fire	Wood	Metal	Water
Metal	Earth	Fire	Water	Wood
Water	Metal	Earth	Wood	Fire

THE FIVE ELEMENTS

ELEMENT	CHARACTERISTICS	PERSONALITIES	ASSOCIATIONS
WOOD	Symbolizes spring, growth and plant life. In its yin form, it is supple and pliable, in its yang form as sturdy as an oak. Positively used, it is a walking stick; negatively used, a spear. Bamboo is cherished in China for its ability to sway in the wind yet be used as scaffolding. Viewed as a tree, Wood energy is expansive, nurturing and versatile.	Wood people are public-spirited and energetic. Ideas people, their outgoing personalities win them support. They visualize rather than committing themselves to plans. *Positively* – they are artistic and undertake tasks with enthusiasm. *Negatively* – they become impatient and angry and often fail to finish the tasks they have begun.	Trees and plants Wooden furniture Paper Green Columns Decking Landscape pictures
FIRE	Symbolizes summer, fire and heat. It can bring light, warmth and happiness or it can erupt, explode and destroy with great violence. Positively, it stands for honour and fairness. Negatively, it stands for aggression and war.	Fire people are leaders and crave action. They inspire others to follow, often into trouble, as they dislike rules and fail to see consequences. *Positively* – they are innovative, humorous and passionate people. *Negatively* – they are impatient, exploit others and have little thought for their feelings.	Sun symbols Candles, lights and lamps Triangles Red Man-made materials Sun or fire pictures
EARTH	Symbolizes the nurturing environment that enables seeds to grow, which all living things emanate from and return to. It nurtures, supports and interacts with each of the other elements. Positively, it denotes fairness, wisdom and instinct. Negatively, it can smother or represent the nervous anticipation of non-existent problems.	Earth people are supportive and loyal. Practical and persevering, they are a tower of strength in a crisis. They do not rush anything, but their support is enduring. Patient and steady, they possess inner strength. *Positively* – earth people are loyal, dependable and patient. *Negatively* – they are obsessional and prone to nit-picking.	Clay, brick and terracotta Cement and stone Squares Yellow, orange and brown
METAL	Symbolizes autumn and strength. Its nature represents solidity and the ability to contain objects. On the other hand, metal is also a conductor. Positively, it represents communication, brilliant ideas and justice. Negatively, it can suggest destruction, danger and sadness. Metal can be a beautiful and precious commodity, or the blade of a weapon.	Metal people are dogmatic and resolute. They pursue their ambitious aims single-mindedly. Good organizers, they are independent and happy in their own company. Faith in their own abilities inclines them towards inflexibility although they thrive on change. They are serious and do not accept help easily. *Positively* – they are strong, intuitive and interesting people. *Negatively* – they are inflexible, melancholic and serious.	All metals Round shapes Domes Metal objects Door furniture and doorsteps Kitchenware White, grey, silver and gold Coins Clocks
WATER	Symbolizes winter and water itself, gentle rain or a storm. It suggests the inner self, art and beauty. It touches everything. Positively, it nurtures and supports with understanding. Negatively, it can wear down and exhaust. Associated with the emotions, it can suggest fear, nervousness and stress.	Water people communicate well. They are diplomatic and persuasive. Sensitive to the moods of others, they will lend an ear. They are intuitive and make excellent negotiators. Flexible and adaptable, they view things holistically. *Positively* – water people are artistic, sociable and sympathetic. *Negatively* – water people are sensitive, fickle and intrusive.	Rivers, streams and lakes Blue and black Mirrors and glass Meandering patterns Fountains and ponds Fish tanks Water pictures

CHINESE ASTROLOGY

An analysis of an environment using a luo pan compass looks at the energetic qualities of the various compass points. The Earthly Branches on the compass represent 12 of these points and also correspond to the 12 animals which relate to Chinese astrology. We often find ourselves in situations at home, or at work, when we canot understand how another person can view the same situation so differently from us, or can make us feel uncomfortable, or find different things irritating or amusing. Looking at the animals enables us to explore these differences by allowing us an insight into the make-up of our natures and personalities.

With this knowledge, we can come to know ourselves better and to accept the personalities of others. At home, it may encourage us to think twice, for instance, before launching into a tirade on tidiness or punctuality. It also has an important use in the workplace in keeping warring factions apart and ensuring a harmonious balance between productive output and socializing.

THE CYCLES

The Chinese calendar is based on the cycle of the moon, which determines that each month is approximately 29½ days long, beginning with a new moon. The years progress in cycles of 12 and it is helpful to appreciate the subtleties of Chinese symbology since each year is represented by an animal and the characteristics of each animal and its way of life are used to identify different types of people. Cultural differences are apt to get in the way if we attempt this identification ourselves; whereas Westerners would describe the Rat's character, for example, as sly and crafty, the Chinese respect its quick mind and native cunning.

In the Chinese calendar each year is represented by an animal and each animal is governed by an element.

Each animal is governed by an element which determines its intrinsic nature. The cycle of 12 is repeated five times to form a larger cycle of 60 years and in each of these cycles, the animals are ascribed an element with either a yin or yang characteristic, which determines their characters. Thus in 60 years, no two animals are the same. We begin by investigating the basic animal characteristics.

If we do not get on with someone, it may be that the animals associated with us in the Chinese calendar are not compatible. Alternatively, it may be that the elements that represent the time of our birth are not in harmony with the elements of the other person.

FINDING YOUR ANIMAL

The Chinese year does not begin on 1st January but on a date which corresponds with the second new moon after the winter equinox, so it varies from year to year. Thus someone born on 25th January 1960 according to the Western calendar would actually be born in 1959 according to the Chinese calendar. The "Chinese Animals Table" opposite gives the exact dates when each year begins and ends, as well as its ruling animal and element. Their outer characteristics are identified by the element of the year they were born, as shown in "The Nature of the Animals" box (left). The ways in which the elements affect an animal's personality are described in "The Five Elements" table.

ANIMAL CYCLES

One of the 12 animals represents each lunar month, each with its own element governing its intrinsic nature. Over 60 years, the Five Elements cycle spins so that each animal can be Wood, Fire, Earth, Metal or Water, which determines its character.

In a full analysis by an experienced Feng Shui consultant, each of us will have a collection of eight elements that together make up not only our character, but also our destiny.

THE NATURE OF THE ANIMALS

Rat	Water
Ox	Earth
Tiger	Wood
Rabbit	Wood
Dragon	Earth
Snake	Fire
Horse	Fire
Goat	Earth
Monkey	Metal
Rooster	Metal
Dog	Earth
Pig	Water

CHINESE ANIMALS TABLE

YEAR	YEAR BEGINS	YEAR ENDS	ANIMAL	ELEMENT	YEAR	YEAR BEGINS	YEAR ENDS	ANIMAL	ELEMENT
1920	20 February 1920	7 February 1921	Monkey	Metal +	1967	9 February 1967	29 January 1968	Goat	Fire −
1921	8 February 1921	27 January 1922	Rooster	Metal −	1968	30 January 1968	16 February 1969	Monkey	Earth +
1922	28 January 1922	15 February 1923	Dog	Water +	1969	17 February 1969	5 February 1970	Rooster	Earth −
1923	16 February 1923	4 February 1924	Pig	Water −	1970	6 February 1970	26 January 1971	Dog	Metal +
1924	5 February 1924	24 January 1925	Rat	Wood +	1971	27 January 1971	15 February 1972	Pig	Metal −
1925	25 January 1925	12 February 1926	Ox	Wood −	1972	16 February 1972	2 February 1973	Rat	Water +
1926	13 February 1926	1 February 1927	Tiger	Fire +	1973	3 February 1973	22 January 1974	Ox	Water −
1927	2 February 1927	22 January 1928	Rabbit	Fire −	1974	23 January 1974	10 February 1975	Tiger	Wood +
1928	23 January 1928	9 February 1929	Dragon	Earth +	1975	11 February 1975	30 January 1976	Rabbit	Wood −
1929	10 February 1929	29 January 1930	Snake	Earth −	1976	31 January 1976	17 February 1977	Dragon	Fire +
1930	30 January 1930	16 February 1931	Horse	Metal +	1977	18 February 1977	6 February 1978	Snake	Fire −
1931	17 February 1931	5 February 1932	Goat	Metal −	1978	7 February 1978	27 January 1979	Horse	Earth +
1932	6 February 1932	25 January 1933	Monkey	Water +	1979	28 January 1979	15 February 1980	Goat	Earth −
1933	26 January 1933	13 February 1934	Rooster	Water −	1980	16 February 1980	4 February 1981	Monkey	Metal +
1934	14 February 1934	3 February 1935	Dog	Wood +	1981	5 February 1981	24 January 1982	Rooster	Metal −
1935	4 February 1935	23 January 1936	Pig	Wood −	1982	25 January 1982	12 February 1983	Dog	Water +
1936	24 January 1936	10 February 1937	Rat	Fire +	1983	13 February 1983	1 February 1984	Pig	Water −
1937	11 February 1937	30 January 1938	Ox	Fire −	1984	2 February 1984	19 February 1985	Rat	Wood +
1938	31 January 1938	18 February 1939	Tiger	Earth +	1985	20 February 1985	8 February 1986	Ox	Wood −
1939	19 February 1939	7 February 1940	Rabbit	Earth −	1986	9 February 1986	28 January 1987	Tiger	Fire +
1940	8 February 1940	26 January 1941	Dragon	Metal +	1987	29 January 1987	16 February 1988	Rabbit	Fire −
1941	27 January 1941	14 February 1942	Snake	Metal −	1988	17 February 1988	5 February 1989	Dragon	Earth +
1942	15 February 1942	4 February 1943	Horse	Water +	1989	6 February 1989	26 January 1990	Snake	Earth −
1943	5 February 1943	24 January 1944	Goat	Water −	1990	27 January 1990	14 February 1991	Horse	Metal +
1944	25 January 1944	12 February 1945	Monkey	Wood +	1991	15 February 1991	3 February 1992	Goat	Metal −
1945	13 February 1945	1 February 1946	Rooster	Wood −	1992	4 February 1992	22 January 1993	Monkey	Water +
1946	2 February 1946	21 January 1947	Dog	Fire +	1993	23 January 1993	9 February 1994	Rooster	Water −
1947	22 January 1947	9 February 1948	Pig	Fire −	1994	10 February 1994	30 January 1995	Dog	Wood +
1948	10 February 1948	28 January 1949	Rat	Earth +	1995	31 January 1995	18 February 1996	Pig	Wood −
1949	29 January 1949	16 February 1950	Ox	Earth −	1996	19 February 1996	6 February 1997	Rat	Fire +
1950	17 February 1950	5 February 1951	Tiger	Metal +	1997	7 February 1997	27 January 1998	Ox	Fire −
1951	6 February 1951	26 January 1952	Rabbit	Metal −	1998	28 January 1998	15 February 1999	Tiger	Earth +
1952	27 January 1952	13 February 1953	Dragon	Water +	1999	16 February 1999	4 February 2000	Rabbit	Earth −
1953	14 February 1953	2 February 1954	Snake	Water −	2000	5 February 2000	23 January 2001	Dragon	Metal +
1954	3 February 1954	23 January 1955	Horse	Wood +	2001	24 January 2001	11 February 2002	Snake	Metal −
1955	24 January 1955	11 February 1956	Goat	Wood −	2002	12 February 2002	31 January 2003	Horse	Water +
1956	12 February 1956	30 January 1957	Monkey	Fire +	2003	1 February 2003	21 January 2004	Goat	Water −
1957	31 January 1957	17 February 1958	Rooster	Fire −	2004	22 January 2004	8 February 2005	Monkey	Wood +
1958	18 February 1958	7 February 1959	Dog	Earth +	2005	9 February 2005	28 January 2006	Rooster	Wood −
1959	8 February 1959	27 January 1960	Pig	Earth −	2006	29 January 2006	17 February 2007	Dog	Fire +
1960	28 January 1960	14 February 1961	Rat	Metal +	2007	18 February 2007	6 February 2008	Pig	Fire −
1961	15 February 1961	4 February 1962	Ox	Metal −	2008	7 February 2008	25 January 2009	Rat	Earth +
1962	5 February 1962	24 January 1963	Tiger	Water +	2009	26 January 2009	13 February 2010	Ox	Earth −
1963	25 January 1963	12 February 1964	Rabbit	Water −	2010	14 February 2010	2 February 2011	Tiger	Metal +
1964	13 February 1964	1 February 1965	Dragon	Wood +	2011	3 February 2011	22 January 2012	Rabbit	Metal −
1965	2 February 1965	20 January 1966	Snake	Wood −	2012	23 January 2012	9 February 2013	Dragon	Water +
1966	21 January 1966	8 February 1967	Horse	Fire +	2013	10 February 2013	30 January 2014	Snake	Water −

THE ANIMAL SIGNS

Using characteristics that are perceived to be an inherent part of the natures of the 12 animals, Chinese astrology attributes certain aspects of these to the characteristics and behaviour of people born at specific times. This system operates in much the same way as Western astrology.

THE RAT

The Rat is an opportunist with an eye for a bargain. Rats tend to collect and hoard, but are unwilling to pay too much for anything. They are devoted to their families, particularly their children. On the surface, Rats are sociable and gregarious yet underneath they can be miserly and petty. Quick-witted and passionate, they are capable of deep emotions despite their cool exteriors. Their nervous energy and ambition may lead Rats to attempt more tasks than they are able to complete successfully. Rats will stand by their friends as long as they receive their support in return. However, they are not above using information given to them in confidence in order to advance their own cause.

▼ *Sociable and family-minded, rats are quick witted and opportunistic.*

▼ *Dependable and loyal, the Ox displays endless patience until pushed too far.*

THE OX

The Ox is solid and dependable. Oxen are excellent organizers and systematic in their approach to every task they undertake. They are not easily influenced by others' ideas. Loyalty is part of their make-up, but if crossed or deceived they will never forget. Oxen do not appear to be imaginative though they are capable of good ideas. Although not demonstrative or the most exciting people romantically, they are entirely dependable

▲ *Dynamic and generous, Tigers are warm-hearted unless they are crossed.*

and make devoted parents. They are people of few words but fine understated gestures. Oxen are renowned for their patience, but it has its limits – once roused, their temper is a sight to behold.

THE TIGER

The Tiger is dynamic, impulsive and lives life to the full. Tigers often leap into projects without planning, but their natural exuberance will carry them through successfully unless boredom creeps in and they do not complete the task. Tigers do not like failure and need to be admired. If their spirits fall, they require a patient ear to listen until they bounce back again. They like excitement in their relationships and static situations leave them cold. Tigers are egotistic. They can be generous and warm, but will also sometimes show their claws.

THE RABBIT

The Rabbit is a born diplomat and cannot bear conflict. Rabbits can be evasive and will often give the answer they think someone wishes to hear rather than enter into a discussion. This is not to say they give in easily: the docile cover hides a strong will and self-assurance. It is difficult to gauge what Rabbits are thinking and they can often appear to be constantly daydreaming, though in reality they may be planning their next strategy. The calmest of the animal signs, Rabbits are social creatures up to the point when their space is invaded. Good communication skills enable Rabbits to enjoy the company of others and they are good counsellors. They prefer to keep away from the limelight where possible and to enjoy the finer things of life.

▲ *Good counsellors and communicators, Rabbits also need their own space.*

THE DRAGON

The Dragon will launch straight into projects or conversations with a pioneering spirit. Dragons often fail to notice others trying to keep up or indeed those plotting behind their backs. Authority figures, they make their own laws and cannot bear restriction. They prefer to get on with a job themselves and are good at motivating others into action.

▲ *Powerful leaders, Dragons prefer to follow their own path in life.*

They are always available to help others, but their pride makes it difficult for them to accept help in return. Although they are always at the centre of things, they tend to be loners and are prone to stress when life becomes difficult. Hard-working and generous, Dragons are entirely trustworthy and are loyal friends. They enjoy excitement and new situations. When upset, they can be explosive, but all is soon forgotten.

THE SNAKE

The Snake is a connoisseur of the good things in life. Inward-looking and self-reliant, Snakes tend to keep their own counsel and dislike relying on others. They can be ruthless in pursuing their goals. Although very kind and generous, Snakes can be demanding in relationships. They find it hard to forgive and will never forget a slight. Never underestimate the patience of a snake, who will wait in the wings until the time is right to strike. They are elegant and sophisticated and although they are good at making money, they never spend it on trifles. Only the best is good enough for them. Very intuitive, Snakes can sense the motives of others and can sum up situations accurately. If crossed, Snakes will bite back with deadly accuracy. They exude an air of mystery, ooze charm and can be deeply passionate.

▼ *Mysterious and passionate, Snakes have endless patience.*

▲ *Active and excitable, the Horse's nervous energy often runs away with them.*

THE HORSE

The Horse is ever-active. Horses will work tirelessly until a project is completed, but only if the deadline is their own. Horses have lightning minds and can sum up people and situations in an instant, sometimes too quickly, and they will move on before seeing the whole picture. Capable of undertaking several tasks at once, Horses are constantly on the move and fond of exercise. They may exhaust themselves physically and mentally. Horses are ambitious and confident in their own abilities. They are not interested in the opinions of others and are adept at side-stepping issues. They can be impatient and have explosive tempers although they rarely bear grudges.

THE GOAT

The Goat is emotional and compassionate. Peace-lovers, Goats always behave correctly and they are extremely accommodating to others. They tend to be shy and vulnerable to criticism. They worry a lot and appear to be easily put upon, but when they feel strongly about something they will dig their heels in and sulk until they achieve their objectives. Goats are generally popular and are usually well cared for by others. They appreciate the finer things in life and are usually lucky. They find it difficult to deal with difficulties and deprivation. Ardent romantics, Goats can obtain their own way by wearing their partners down and turning every occasion to their advantage. They will do anything to avoid conflict and hate making decisions.

▼ *Peace-loving Goats are kind and popular, they hate conflict and will try to avoid it.*

THE MONKEY

The Monkey is intelligent and capable of using its wits to solve problems. Monkeys often wriggle out of difficult situations and are not above trickery if it will further their own ends. Monkeys tend to be oblivious of other people and of the effect their own actions may have on them. In spite of this, they are usually popular and are able to motivate others by their sheer enthusiasm for new projects. Monkeys are constantly on the look out for new challenges and their innovative approach and excellent memories generally make them successful. They are full of energy and are always active. They have little sympathy for those who are unable to keep up with them, but will soon forget any difficulties.

▼ *Energetic Monkeys use their intelligence to push their own ideas forward.*

▲ *The flamboyant Rooster can be easily won over by flattery and admiration.*

THE ROOSTER

The Rooster is a very sociable creature. Roosters shine in situations where they are able to be the centre of attention. If a Rooster is present, everyone will be aware of the fact because no Rooster can ever take a back seat at a social gathering. They are dignified, confident and extremely strong-willed, yet they may have a negative streak. They excel in arguments and debates. Incapable of underhandedness, Roosters lay all their cards on the table and do not spare others' feelings in their quest to do the right thing. They never weary of getting to the bottom of a problem and are perfectionists in all that they do. Roosters can usually be won over by flattery. Full of energy, Roosters are brave, but they hate criticism and can be puritanical in their approach to life.

THE DOG

The Dog is entirely dependable and has an inherent sense of justice. Intelligent, Dogs are loyal to their friends and they always listen to the problems of others, although they can be critical. In a crisis, Dogs will always help and they will never betray a friend. They can be hard workers, but are

▼ *Dogs are loyal and hard-working, but enjoy relaxing too.*

not all that interested in accumulating wealth for themselves. They like to spend time relaxing. Dogs take time to get to know people but have a tendency to pigeon-hole them. When they want something badly they can be persistent. If roused they can be obstinate and occasionally they lash out, although their temper is usually short-lived. Some Dogs can be rather nervous and they may be prone to pessimism.

▲ *Peace-loving Pigs are sociable and popular and are able to organize others well.*

THE PIG

The Pig is everybody's friend. Honest and generous, Pigs are always available to bail others out of difficulties. Pigs love the social scene and are popular. They rarely argue and if they do fly off the handle, they bear no grudges afterwards. They abhor conflict and very often will not notice when others are attempting to upset them. They prefer to think well of people. Over-indulgence is their greatest weakness and Pigs will spend heavily in pursuit of pleasure. They always share with their friends and trust that, in return, their friends will make allowances for their own little weaknesses. Great organizers, Pigs like to have a cause and will often rally others to it as well.

COMPATIBILITY OF SIGNS

The saying, "You can choose your friends but not your family", is often heard from those who do not have harmonious family relationships, and we all find that we are drawn more to some people than to others. Chinese astrology uses the year, month, day and time of birth (each of which is represented by an animal and the yin or yang attributes of its accompanying element) to analyse characters and predict fortunes. Analyses of relationships depend upon the interaction of the elements on each person's chart. We can gain some insight into our

▼ *We are drawn to people for a variety of reasons. Compatibility of animal signs and elements can certainly help.*

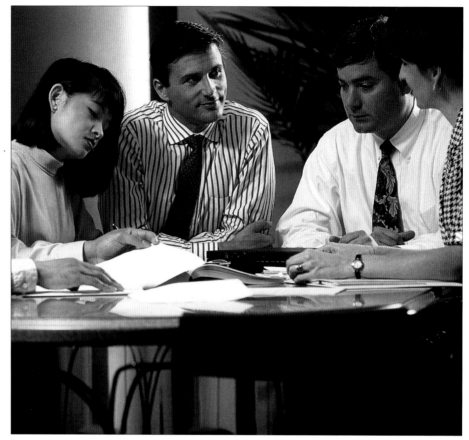

own characters and those of our family and colleagues by using the "Chinese Animals Table" and then looking at the associated elements with their yang (+) (positive characteristics) or yin (−) (negative characteristics) in "The Five Elements" table.

▲ *We function well at work when we are compatible with our colleagues. The man on the right looks uncomfortable.*

▼ *This table shows which of our family, friends and colleagues we relate to best according to Chinese astrology.*

COMPATIBILITY TABLE

	RAT	OX	TIGER	RABBIT	DRAGON	SNAKE	HORSE	GOAT	MONKEY	ROOSTER	DOG	PIG
RAT	+	=	+	−	★	=	−	−	★	−	+	+
OX	=	+	−	=	+	★	−	−	+	★	−	+
TIGER	+	−	+	−	+	−	★	+	−	=	★	=
RABBIT	+	+	−	+	=	+	−	★	−	−	=	★
DRAGON	★	−	+	=	−	+	+	+	★	+	+	=
SNAKE	+	★	−	+	=	+	+	=	−	★	+	−
HORSE	−	−	★	−	=	+	−	=	+	+	★	+
GOAT	−	−	=	★	+	+	=	+	+	−	−	★
MONKEY	★	+	−	−	★	−	−	+	=	+	+	=
ROOSTER	−	★	+	−	=	★	+	=	−	−	+	+
DOG	+	−	★	=	−	+	★	−	+	+	=	+
PIG	=	+	=	★	+	−	−	★	−	+	+	−

KEY: ★ Excellent = Good + Workable − Difficult

THE ANIMAL YEARS

As we have seen, each year is ruled by an animal and its character is said to denote the energetic quality of the year.

The animal which rules each year and the date of the Chinese New Year for around a hundred-year period are shown on the "Chinese Animals Table". For ease of reference, 1999–2010 are shown below. Our fortunes in each year are indicated by whether or not we are compatible with the animal ruling that year, which can be checked by referring back to the "Compatibility Table".

1999	Rabbit	2005	Rooster
2000	Dragon	2006	Dog
2001	Snake	2007	Pig
2002	Horse	2008	Rat
2003	Goat	2009	Ox
2004	Monkey	2010	Tiger

YEAR OF THE RABBIT
A respite from the past year and a breather before the next, rest is indicated here. This is a time for negotiations and settlements, but not for new ventures. Women's and family concerns are considered important.

YEAR OF THE DRAGON
The time for new business ventures and projects. Euphoric and unpredictable, this is the year for outlandish schemes and taking risks. Dragon babies are considered lucky.

YEAR OF THE SNAKE
Peace returns and allows time to reflect. Care should be taken in business matters as treachery and underhand dealings are indicated. Money is made and communication is good. A fertile year, in which morality becomes an issue.

YEAR OF THE HORSE
An energetic and volatile year in which money will be spent and borrowed. Some impulsive behaviour will bring rewards, while some will fail. A year for marriage and divorce.

YEAR OF THE GOAT
A quiet year in which family matters are to the fore. A year for consolidating and for diplomatic negotiations, rather than launching new projects.

YEAR OF THE MONKEY
An unpredictable year when nothing goes according to plan. Only the quick-witted will prosper. New ideas abound and communication will flourish.

YEAR OF THE ROOSTER
A year for making feelings known and letting grievances out. This may cause disharmony in families so tact is required.

YEAR OF THE DOG
Worthy causes abound – human and animal rights and environmental issues are in the public eye. Security should be checked, by governments and at home. A year for marriage and the family.

YEAR OF THE PIG
The last year of the cycle and unfinished business should be concluded. Optimism abounds and the pursuit of leisure is indicated. Family concerns will go well.

YEAR OF THE RAT
This is a lucky year, a good time to start a new venture. The rewards will not come without hard work, but with careful planning they will arrive.

YEAR OF THE OX
Harvest is the symbol for this year so we will reap what we have sown. Decisions should be made now and contracts signed. This is a conservative year so grand or outrageous schemes are not considered appropriate.

YEAR OF THE TIGER
Sudden conflicts and crises arise in this year and will have an impact for some time. The year for grand schemes for the courageous, but underhand activities may suffer from repercussions.

▼ *Family relationships are usually harmonious if the animal signs are compatible and the elements do not clash.*

THE BAGUA AND THE MAGIC SQUARE

The compass directions and their associations are fundamental to the practice of Feng Shui. Astronomical and geomantic calculations and the place of human beings within them are plotted on a luo pan, an instrument so powerful that it has been likened to a computer. The luo pan can indicate, to those who know how to interpret it, which illness someone in a certain location might be suffering from, or the fortunes of a person living in a certain room in a house.

This vast amount of information has been reduced to a shorthand form incorporated in a "Magic Square". In cultures worldwide, this was used as a talisman. Many formulae based on the magic square are used to discover whether a place is auspicious, in itself and for the people living there, and the simplest of these are introduced in this book. The diagram on the right shows how the energies represented by the Magic Square always move in a fixed pattern. These patterns are repeated over time and can indicate the fortunes of a person or building in a certain year.

THE BAGUA

The information contained in the luo pan is condensed into the Magic Square, which forms the basis of the Bagua, or Pa Kua, a tool we can use to investigate our homes and offices. The Bagua below holds some of the images which describe the energies of the eight directions and the central position. The Bagua represents the journey of life, the Tao, and we can use it to create comfortable living, working and leisure spaces.

When applying Feng Shui principles to your house, garden or office you will need a tracing of the Bagua with the colours, compass points and directions all added on.

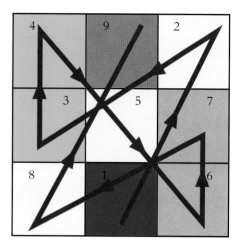

▲ *The Magic Square: the "magic" lies in the fact that every line adds up to 15. Magic squares exist all over the world. In ancient cultures, such symbols were a source of power to their initiates. In Hebrew culture, the pattern formed by the movement of energies is known as the seal of Saturn and is used in Western magic. In Islamic cultures, intricate patterns are based on complex magic squares.*

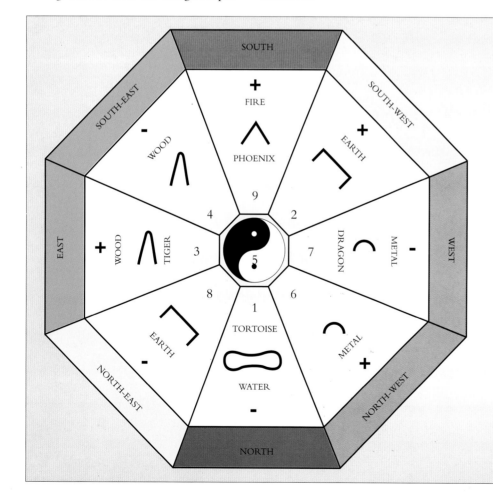

THE BAGUA, OR PA KUA

This diagram shows the energies associated with each of the eight directions. The outer bar shows the colours and directions associated with the five elements. The symbols indicate the yin (-) or yang (+) quality of the element associated with each direction. Also shown are the shapes associated with each element. The four symbolic animals which represent the energy of each of the four cardinal directions – north, south, east, west – are indicated, and the numbers of the Magic Square are shown in their associated directions. We take on the characteristics of a number and the energies associated with it, which are thought to shape who we are, where we feel comfortable, and our fortunes. The Chinese compass is always drawn facing south since this is the favoured direction for houses to face in parts of China. This does not affect the actual magnetic north-south directions.

FINDING YOUR MAGIC NUMBER

To complete the picture, it is necessary to discover how human beings fit into the scheme. Each person is allocated a "magic" number that enables them to position themselves to their best advantage. Before finding our number from the tables opposite, we must check the date of the Chinese New Year from the "Chinese Animals Table". The previous year is used if our birthday falls before the start of the new year.

▼ *Each of the magic numbers represents a particular type of energy suggested by the annual nature cycle. Find your number on the table and discover your energy below.*

ENERGY OF NUMBERS

1: Water. Winter. Independent.
   Intuitive
2: Earth. Late Summer. Methodical.
3: Thunder. Spring. Progressive
4: Wind. Late Spring. Adaptable.
5: Earth. Central Force. Assertive.
6: Heaven. Late Autumn. Unyielding.
7: Lake. Autumn. Flexible. Nervous.
8: Mountain. Late Winter. Obstinate.
   Energetic.
9: Fire. Summer. Impulsive.
   Intelligent.

USING THE MAGIC NUMBERS

Some Feng Shui consultants use only the male, or yang, numbers in their calculations, some use both male and female, or yin, numbers. Others regard the yin (female) numbers as depicting the inner self, while the yang (male) numbers represent the image a person presents to the world. Traditional male and female stereotypes are no longer the norm. Modern men and women, with more interchangeable roles, tend to have both yin and yang characteristics.

EAST-WEST DIRECTIONS

People tend to fare better in some directions than in others. They fall into two groups, the east group or the west group. Those who fall into the east group should live in a house facing an east group direction, those in the west group a west group direction. If this is not possible, your bed and/or your chair should face an appropriate direction.

▼ *Once you have found your magic number, you can identify which group you are in, east or west, which directions suit you. and whether your house is compatible.*

GROUP	NUMBERS	DIRECTIONS
East	1, 3, 4, 9	N, E, SE, S
West	2, 5, 6, 7, 8	SW, NW, W, NE, CENTRE

THE MAGIC NUMBERS

YEAR	M	F	YEAR	M	F	YEAR	M	F	YEAR	M	F
1920	8	7	1952	3	3	1984	7	8	2002	7	8
1921	7	8	1953	2	4	1985	6	9	2003	6	9
1922	6	9	1954	1	5	1986	5	1	2004	5	1
1923	5	1	1955	9	6	1987	4	2	2005	4	2
1924	4	2	1956	8	7	1988	3	3	2006	3	3
1925	3	3	1957	7	8	1989	2	4	2007	2	4
1926	2	4	1958	6	9	1990	1	5	2008	1	5
1927	1	5	1959	5	1	1991	9	6	2009	9	6
1928	9	6	1960	4	2	1992	8	7	2010	8	7
1929	8	7	1961	3	3	1993	7	8	2011	7	8
1930	7	8	1962	2	4	1994	6	9	2012	6	9
1931	6	9	1963	1	5	1995	5	1	2013	5	1
1932	5	1	1964	9	6	1996	4	2	2014	4	2
1933	4	2	1965	8	7	1997	3	3	2015	3	3
1934	3	3	1966	7	8	1998	2	4	2016	2	4
1935	2	4	1967	6	9	1999	1	5	2017	1	5
1936	1	5	1968	5	1	2000	9	6	2018	9	6
1937	9	6	1969	4	2	2001	8	7	2019	8	7
1938	8	7	1970	3	3						
1939	7	8	1971	2	4						
1940	6	9	1972	1	5						
1941	5	1	1973	9	6						
1942	4	2	1974	8	7						
1943	3	3	1975	7	8						
1944	2	4	1976	6	9						
1945	1	5	1977	5	1						
1946	9	6	1978	4	2						
1947	8	7	1979	3	3						
1948	7	8	1980	2	4						
1949	6	9	1981	1	5						
1950	5	1	1982	9	6						
1951	4	2	1983	8	7						

Key: M = male F = female

▼ *A Chinese Feng Shui expert studies the luo pan (compass).*

PERCEPTION AND THE SYMBOLIC BAGUA

Much of the skill in undertaking a Feng Shui survey of our immediate environment is in reading the signals there. If we are healthy and happy, this may prove to be a comparatively easy process. If we are not, our perception may be coloured by our emotional or physical state and we may not be able to see things clearly.

The Chinese phrase "First, luck; second, destiny; third, Feng Shui; fourth, virtues; fifth, education" is worth repeating, as it shows that to some extent our fortunes and personalities are out of our hands. If we embrace Feng Shui, think and act positively, and make use of the knowledge the universe has to offer, then we can begin to take charge of the parts of our lives that we can control and make the best of them.

Part of the process of Feng Shui is to awaken our senses and sensibilities to our environment. Among other things, each of the Five Elements governs different senses, and our aim is to create a balanced environment in which all our senses are satisfied and none is allowed to predominate over the rest to create an imbalance.

We can heighten our perception of the world if we introduce ourselves to different experiences. Take an objective look at your weekly routine and decide on a new experience or activity which will add something different to your life.

A MAGICAL TEMPLATE

When Feng Shui began to take off in the West several years ago, the workings of the compass were known only to a handful of scholars. Those early days were distinguished by the creation of, and endless discussions on, the workings of the Bagua. It was used then, as it is now, by the Tibetan Black Hat practitioners, as a magical template that is aligned with a front door, the entrance to a room, the front of a desk or even a face.

This template is then used to supply information which can enable us to understand our energy and make corrections to create balance and harmony. Some Chinese practitioners have since

A HEALTHY LIFESTYLE AND A HEALTHY MIND

Stuck energy in our homes is often a reflection of our lifestyle and state of mind. A healthy daily regime will make us receptive to the powers of Feng Shui.

Ideally, we should take time out each day to meditate – or just to escape from stress. Often a short walk, gardening or a few minutes sitting quietly will help us to relax. Holidays and new experiences can help our mental energy.

Chi Kung and T'ai Chi are part of the same system. Their exercise programmes help to keep the energy channels in the body unblocked, while also releasing the mind.

Eating a healthy balanced diet of food-stuffs, produced without chemical interference, is another way of ensuring that harmful energies, or toxins, do not upset our bodily balance.

If we do become ill, acupuncture and acupressure and Chinese herbal medicine can balance the energies in our bodies and help to keep us fit.

◀ *Meditation (left), hiking in the mountains (bottom left) or a daily session of T'ai Chi (bottom right) will all benefit our mental energy and help to heighten our perceptions.*

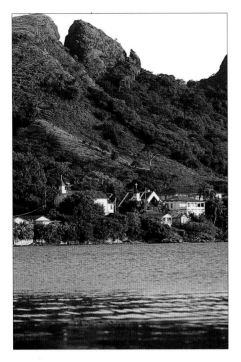

▲ *Mountains afford protection to the rear and sides of this village, while a lake in front accumulates chi – all that remains is to arrange the inside of the house to create a supportive environment.*

sought to use the Bagua alongside the compass method. They place it over the plan of a home so that it is positioned with the Career area in the north, irrespective of where the front door lies.

Other traditional Chinese approaches concentrate on interpreting the energies indicated by the Five Elements and by the rings of the luo pan. Such is the "magic" of Feng Shui that, in the right hands, all approaches appear to work.

Newcomers to Feng Shui may find it difficult to connect to a compass. Hopefully, they will use either method to experience for themselves the magic of the early days of discovery, and will be drawn deeper into this amazing philosophy, gaining an insight into its power.

▼ *The Three Gates Bagua. This may be entered through "Career" (back), "Knowledge" (bottom left) or "Helpful People" (bottom right). The compass Bagua with associated colours is shown inside to help you balance the elements of your home.*

THE SYMBOLIC BAGUA

Throughout this book we will see how various images are connected to each of the eight points of the Magic Square or the Bagua, which is based on it. The symbolic Bagua uses the energies of each direction to relate to the journey of life. The journey begins at the entrance to our home – the mouth of chi – and moves in a predetermined way through the home until it reaches its conclusion. By focusing on an aspect of our lives which we want to stimulate or change, we can use the energies of the universe and make them work for us. Psychologically, focusing on an area enables us to create the circumstances to bring about change.

So far, a traditional compass approach has been used, but the diagram to the left allows us to use either approach. From now on readers should feel free to connect with the Bagua as they wish, and through it to the intangible forces which make this such a fascinating subject. Most people who have used Feng Shui have experienced changes in their circumstances. These often correspond to the actual energy around a relationship or situation rather than our desires. The results will ultimately serve our best interests, but the outcome is often unexpected.

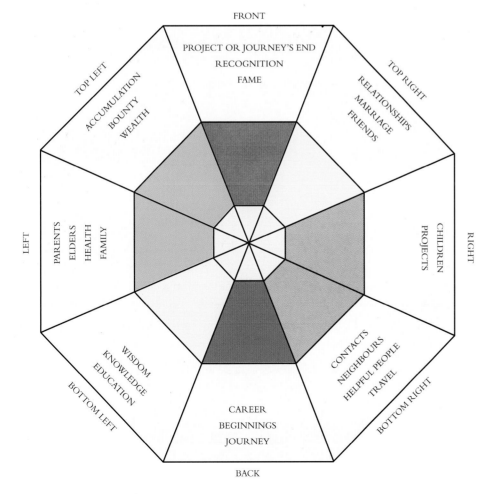

FRONT

PROJECT OR JOURNEY'S END
RECOGNITION
FAME

TOP LEFT

ACCUMULATION
BOUNTY
WEALTH

TOP RIGHT

RELATIONSHIPS
MARRIAGE
FRIENDS

LEFT

PARENTS
ELDERS
HEALTH
FAMILY

RIGHT

CHILDREN
PROJECTS

WISDOM
KNOWLEDGE
EDUCATION

BOTTOM LEFT

CAREER
BEGINNINGS
JOURNEY

CONTACTS
NEIGHBOURS
HELPFUL PEOPLE
TRAVEL

BOTTOM RIGHT

BACK

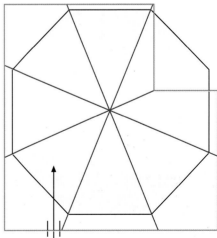

▲ *The Three Gates Bagua is flexible. If a home has an irregular shape, the corresponding area of the Bagua is also considered to be missing. In this house, the front entrance is in the "Knowledge" area and the "Relationships" part of the house is missing.*

FENG SHUI IN THE MODERN WORLD

Modern lifestyles are far removed from those of our ancestors. For them, charting the progress of the moon and sun, and interpreting the different weather conditions and other activities occurring in the natural world in relation to the movement of the stars and planets,

▼ *There are still thriving cultures in which ancient skills and lifestyles remain such as this village in Chad.*

▲ *Night-time in Mexico City. The 23 million inhabitants are denied a view of the stars because of neon lighting and pollution.*

▶ *The rice harvest in traditional regions of China has used many of the same processes for the past thousand years.*

was essential. These peoples depended on the land to provide them with the means to survive. The modern city-dweller may never see food growing naturally and may not even be able to view the night sky because of pollution and neon lighting. However, we still depend on the natural world for our well-being. We can be at the mercy of hurricanes, or bask on sun-drenched beaches; mountains may erupt, or provide sustenance for livestock; human beings can pollute the air and contaminate the land, or create sanctuaries for wildlife species.

Ancient peoples, through necessity, regarded the heavens, the earth and themselves as part of one system. This holistic view of life has persisted in many cultures, where health and medicine, food and lifestyle are all interconnected. In the West, scientific development created different disciplines which advanced in isolation from each other. Through recent movements in health and food production, we are seeking to correct the imbalances caused by this approach. The Tao, or the Way, the philosophy which underlies Feng Shui, shows how it is possible to order our lives to exist in harmony with each other and the natural world. We can use Feng Shui to help us work towards achieving this.

The traditional concept of Gaia, the Greek earth goddess, was used by James Lovelock and Lynne Margulis in the 1970s to encourage us to perceive the world as a biosphere in which each constituent part has a role to play. In order to understand Feng Shui we need to expand this concept of ecosystems further to include human beings and the impact of

▲ *In 1948 science writer Fred Hoyle predicted: "Once a photograph of the Earth taken from the outside world is available … a new idea as powerful as any other in history will be let loose." The environmental awareness movement began at the time human beings landed on the moon.*

WORKING WITH THE NATURAL WORLD

A good example of working with the natural world is provided by an apparently admirable scheme to plant 300 oak forests in Britain to celebrate the millennium. But in the natural world oak trees grow singly and not in rows in large groups, and recent research has indicated that where many oaks grow together there is a higher incidence of Lyme disease, a debilitating illness which attacks the nervous system. The reason for this is that mice and deer feed on acorns and also carry the ticks which transmit the disease. Thus, where there are many oaks, there is also a high

incidence of Lyme disease. Mixed planting, which mirrors the natural world, would be preferable.

In order to save money, one forest was planted with Polish oak trees that came into bud two weeks later than the native trees. This meant there were no caterpillars feeding on the buds to provide food for newly-hatched fledglings. These mistakes might have been avoided if Taoistic principles had been applied to the scheme.

▼ *Native trees act as the Tortoise, Dragon, Tiger formation to protect these buildings.*

the cosmos, and to expand our awareness so that we can predict the consequences of our actions.

As we investigate the ideas behind Feng Shui and consider practical ways of introducing them into our lives, we also need to shift our perception. Feng Shui in the modern world incorporates intuition. Maori warriors navigate hundreds of miles by the feel of a place and by observing signs. The Inuit language incorporates many words to describe the complexities of different types of snow. Similarly, we can heighten our awareness of our environment by adopting the principles of Feng Shui.

Until recently navigators used the stars to steer by, and in some parts of the world those who work with the land still use the stars to determine planting times for their crops. These people recognize patterns in the interrelationship between different parts of the natural world, noticing which plants are in flower or when birds return from migration and comparing them to the weather. Many customs are firmly based in natural wisdom.

THE FENG SHUI OFFICE

MANY OF US SPEND A LARGE PART OF OUR LIVES
AT WORK AND OUR SURROUNDINGS THERE ARE
AS IMPORTANT AS THOSE IN OUR HOMES. WE
USUALLY HAVE LITTLE CONTROL OVER THE
BUILDINGS WE WORK IN, BUT AWARENESS OF
PROBLEMS THAT CAN AFFECT US WILL ENABLE US
TO TAKE COUNTER-MEASURES AND MAY
ENCOURAGE THE CREATION OF STIMULATING
AND NURTURING ENVIRONMENTS.

INTRODUCTION

The Feng Shui principles are "First, luck; second, destiny; third, Feng Shui; fourth, virtues; fifth, education". While we have no control over our luck or our destiny, we can have an impact on the quality of our lives by applying ourselves to the other three areas. Education in childhood may vary in quality but as we get older we are able to take more responsibility for it. We are privileged if our early education is of a high standard and enables us to acquire the knowledge and skills needed to enhance our careers,

▼ *The energy of an office is dependent on the people who work there, and the relationships they form with each other.*

▲ *In this clutter-free and airy office, there is room for personal space and a central meeting point.*

▶ *In this modern office, meeting areas again combine with individual spaces to give a harmonious working environment.*

but we should also take steps to improve our knowledge and expertise when we are adults. The term "virtues" applies to the way we relate to people and situations. How we relate to people is, to some extent, written in our horoscopes, but our own personal energy also plays a large part. We can also apply Feng Shui to create an environment which will support us and enable us to make progress.

The energy of any office can be dramatically improved if its occupants respond to each other in a positive way and co-operate with one another. If the office environment is unsatisfactory, it is possible to offer to paint it and to move in plants and images which will improve it and make it a better place to work. If the management is considered to be unreasonable and deadlines are unrealis-

tic, there should be a way of approaching a situation positively to avoid conflict. Negativity breeds negativity so forward planning and planning work programmes holistically, rather than on a day-to-day basis, will reduce stress.

Our relationships with our colleagues will influence our happiness and performance at work. Astrology plays a part in determining our characteristics and those of the people we have positive and negative relationships with. Understanding this will benefit us and help us to create harmony in the office or workspace.

The location of the office is not normally something over which we have control but its internal layout can make a great difference to the way people feel and behave. It is now thought that some buildings are "sick" and an awareness of the causes can improve the lot of those who work there. When we employ Feng Shui in an office environment we can assist the movement of the energies and at the very least we can take positive steps to keep our personal workspace clear of an accumulation of clutter which will affect our performance.

It is accepted that the energies of home and workplace are not independent of each other and if something is not working well in one, it will affect the other. If relationships at home are not happy, it could be because of a problem in the office, which could be caused by a lack of harmonious relationships there, or the problem could simply be a blockage of chi resulting from the position of a desk or workstation.

Feng Shui can help in the office environment in two ways. It can help to make the business function efficiently and prosper; to gain an advantage over competitors, as it is widely used in the East; and to give individuals the edge over rivals in career development – all yang aspects. The second, yin, application is to improve job satisfaction, foster harmonious working relationships, and provide a stress-free environment in which personal careers can develop and the company can thrive.

FENG SHUI IN PRACTICE

The plans for the famous Hong Kong and Shanghai Bank in Hong Kong, designed by British architect Sir Norman Foster, required modification before it was considered suitable by a local Feng Shui consultant. Detail on the outside of the building was altered so that the symbolic arrows point up and not down as on the original plan. The escalators

▲ *The Hong Kong and Shanghai Bank stands in a prime position facing Victoria harbour and is protected behind by the Peak, one of the Dragon Hills that protect Hong Kong.*

were realigned to draw chi into the building from an auspicious direction and the large stone lions which protect the entrance were placed in position at an auspicious time.

The bank's main rival, the Bank of China, erected a new building soon afterwards and started a Feng Shui war. The new building's design was such that its corners directed "poison arrows" of negative energy at its rival, who had to ward it off by installing mirrored glass to symbolically direct it back again.

Another aggressive measure in the East is to point cannons at rivals, who respond by installing larger ones to point back.

EXTERNAL FACTORS

—

*The buildings we inhabit are part of a wider
environment that can have a profound effect on how we
operate within them. Their location, what they are
surrounded with and even their shape can make us feel
comfortable, or it can jar and can have a great impact on
our clients. The energy emanating from different directions
suits some businesses more than others and we can design
our office space in order to encourage these different
energies. When we move to a new building, or travel,
the timing is crucial to the success of the venture.*

LOCATION

When you are searching for suitable business premises there are important questions to ask even before finding out about access and other practical matters. A walk around the area will indicate if it is thriving or not and what type of activities are located there. The fortunes of the previous occupants can provide a clue to how successful the new undertaking will be, and it is worth making enquiries as to their activities and how they fared before committing yourself to a building or area.

The maxim, "Location is everything" applies to offices as well as houses. A prestigious address may be taken as a sign of success by clients who may not realize that your office is little more than a cupboard on a floor shared by three other companies, but a company operating in such a space would not thrive for long unless other factors were right. Some areas are traditionally associated with certain types of business – for example, lawyers. Support networks spring up,

▼ *The water and greenery around this building, appropriately home of a building design company, help to energize its environment.*

▲ *The varied skyline of downtown San Francisco indicates a thriving and successful city, full of business opportunities.*

contacts are made in cafés during lunch breaks and in bars after office hours, and other enterprises which are not associated will feel isolated. One question which needs to be asked by organizations on the move, or those setting up, is whether or not the area really needs the

services it is offering. There are only so many solicitors, estate agents or expensive boutiques that one area can support, and in many cases the success of a business is down to market research and is not something that Feng Shui can cure.

Sometimes we have an impractical dream of setting up a business or opening a shop offering a service or products which the area does not need. For example, a sushi bar in a district predominantly populated by low-income families with small children will not thrive since the food tends to be expensive, such families have to budget carefully and young children are notoriously unadventurous when it comes to diet. A themed diner-type establishment offering burgers and fries and catering for children's parties would probably thrive in such an area. Similarly, a shop selling modern craftwork and ethnic jewellery is unlikely to do well in an area where the population is elderly. Market research is well worth doing before establishing a business and a little research initially may prevent problems later.

It is true that the fortunes of locations run in cycles but, even so, an area which is run down, where vegetation does not thrive, and where there are many empty or vandalized buildings is best avoided. It is often possible to read patterns into the energy of an environment or a particular building. If a building has had a fire, then it pays to be wary. If the previous occupants of a building were in a similar line

of business and went bankrupt, or had to reduce their activities drastically, warning bells should ring. It may have been due to poor management, but it could also be associated with the building and its environment. In either case, potential clients may associate the two businesses so it

▲ *Water is good for communications, but some Wood and Fire energy is also needed for this book-supplying company. At present the Earth element dominates.*

would be better to steer clear. It is recognized in Feng Shui that certain types of business thrive in certain types of building and location. Choosing the correct ones for a business is the first step on the road to success.

▼ *This restaurant will thrive – the colours and seating are designed for a quick turnover of people in a bustling city location.*

THE FIVE ELEMENTS AND BUILDINGS

Buildings and environments associated with each of the Five Elements support different types of business activity.

ELEMENT	TYPE OF BUILDING, ENVIRONMENT AND ENERGY	SUITABLE BUSINESSES
WOOD	Wood buildings are tall and narrow in shape, or are made of wood. Wood environments are ones where there are trees and vegetation. The energy suggests new ideas and new beginnings.	Woodcrafts, Garden centres, Artists, New businesses, Products
FIRE	Fire buildings have pointed roofs and spires. Fire environments may have chimneys. The energy suggests production and dynamism.	Manufacturing, PR and marketing, Sales
EARTH	Earth buildings are rectangular and have flat roofs. Earth environments tend to be flat and fenced. The energy suggests stability, nourishment and nurture.	Storage and warehousing, Agriculture, Housing
METAL	Metal buildings tend to be round or domed. Metal environments are those where fuels, minerals and gases are extracted from the earth. The energy suggests consolidation and profit.	Metal crafts, Jewellery, Mining, Finance
WATER	Water buildings are those which have irregular shapes. Water environments are ones suggesting flow and making links. The energy is that of communication.	Communications, Electrical systems, Liquids, Healing

THE OFFICE SITUATION

Where offices are situated and the support they receive from other buildings are crucial. Open communication channels and access are also very important to the success of a business.

THE FOUR DIRECTIONS

The first consideration when choosing an office location is support and we can apply the Four Animals arrangement here. Although it is not considered good Feng Shui for an office to be dwarfed by surrounding buildings, it is useful if there is a taller building to the rear to act as the Tortoise, with supportive buildings on either side: the Dragon, to the right when facing the building, should be higher than the Tiger on the left. Alternatively, trees or (for lower buildings) walls and fences, can fulfil these roles.

In the Phoenix position, at the front of the building, it is important to mark the front boundary of the business in

▲ *In Feng Shui terms, round-edged buildings are more sociable than square-edged buildings.*

▼ *This building would benefit from having railings right across the front and lowering the wall to give an even view.*

some way, with a low wall or fence, or with a sign carrying the company name. If a tall barrier is needed for security reasons, choose railings rather than a solid wall or fence. This allows a view from the building whereas a solid barrier would be restricting. Since it enables others to see in, it will also offer more security against break-ins.

Having found a good position to locate your business, it is important to check for any threatening features in the environment. The corners of adjacent or opposing buildings, glare from glass buildings and satellite dishes, and flag poles or decorative features pointing at the office are all of concern since they appear to attack us.

ACCESS

In ancient times, rivers were the main routes of access. Today roads and other transport links serve the same purpose

▲ *Hong Kong harbour accumulates chi for the island and helps to create prosperity for the many businesses located there.*

and their importance in the siting of business premises will depend on the nature of the business, the numbers of visitors, deliveries and so on. A company which uses technology as its main communication channel will not be so dependent on roads. Whatever the nature of the business, it is important that its communication channels are kept open. Poor service from network providers and computer engineers to such a business is the equivalent of unreliable rail links and road systems to others.

Businesses situated on urban freeways will suffer if they have frequent visitors and deliveries but do not have adequate parking facilities. Those situated by roundabouts rarely do well since traffic, or chi, is constantly passing by, unable to stop or collect there. Buildings located at crossroads, on the other hand, are considered to have good Feng Shui, since traffic approaches them from two directions. However, this is diminished if there are other buildings pointing at them from the diagonally opposite corner. A mirror, or other reflective surface, will direct the negative energy back at itself.

Buildings at the end of a T-junction, with traffic travelling straight towards them, are seen to be under threat and

▲ *Stunning foliage helps to provide a vibrant energy for an international western company in this Malaysian suburb.*

▼ *The green area around these office buildings provides some protection from the Lyndon Johnson Freeway in Dallas, USA.*

▲ *The Johannesburg Stock Exchange depends entirely on efficient communication channels and can only thrive if these are working well.*

those in a peninsula position are considered to be unstable. A cul-de-sac location is not generally considered to be good Feng Shui, since parking will almost certainly be restricted and the energy will become stuck.

Wherever possible, attempt to create a well-maintained garden or green area around the building, which will be attractive to workers and visitors alike and will provide a barrier between the office and the road.

HARNESSING THE ENERGIES

Feng Shui considers that different types of energies emanate from each direction. Since it is based on the cycles of nature, it is easy to understand that, for example, the energy of the east is represented by the rising sun and by spring and fresh young growth. If we employ this imagery we can see that the rising energy of the east would suit new companies; the south, dynamic activities such as marketing; the west, consolidation and financial activities; and the more static northern energy, activities indicating stillness such as storage or counselling.

The energy of your business is primarily determined by the direction in which the entrance faces.

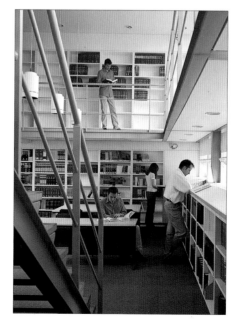

▲ *This designer's home and studio symbolize the Wood element – it even looks as if a tree is growing through the centre.*

◄ *Libraries and archives are ideal in the north, which symbolizes storage and communication activities.*

YIN AND YANG

We can utilize the principles of Feng Shui to help us determine the types of activities which will be suitable in each direction. The Bagua diagram indicates the elements associated with the directions, and which of them are considered to have yin qualities and which have yang attributes.

WOOD: Often known as "The Arousing" in its yang form, Wood signifies growth and movement. In its yang form it is more dynamic, suggesting brainstorming, new ideas and snap decisions. In its yin form, often referred to as "The Penetrating", it is more intuitive. Plans are carried forward and executed, ideas turned into designs.

YIN (–) SOUTH-EAST: Design
YANG (+) EAST: Development, ideas

METAL: In its yin form, Metal is known as "The Joyous". It suggests pleasure and reflection, both in its inward and outward manifestations, mirrors and shiny objects, and contemplation. In its yang form, Metal is often referred to as "The Creative" and suggests strength and immobility as represented by large manufacturing machinery.

YIN (–) WEST: Small metal objects, e.g. knives, ornaments, finance, meditation
YANG (+) NORTH-WEST: Heavy engineering, machinery

EARTH: In its yin form, Earth is often known as "The Mountain", indicating stillness. Here we sow the seeds, prepare and provide support. In its yang form, Earth is often referred to as "The Receptive" and is productive – its output is turned into goods.

YIN (–) NORTH-EAST: Plant nurseries, printing and reprographic services
YANG (+) SOUTH-WEST: Quarrying, pottery, food production

FIRE: Fire is yang and does not have a yin form. It is also known as "The Clinging" and suggests activities concerned with bringing ideas and products to fruition and promoting them.

YANG (+) SOUTH: publishing, public relations, laboratories

▲ *Laboratories do well in the south, symbolized by the Fire element.*

WATER: Water is yin and does not have a yang form. It is also known as "The Abysmal" and suggests an area where the energy is not active, but where there is a regular flow.

YIN (–) NORTH: Storage and warehousing, secret negotiations, production lines

◀ *The Metal energy of the west is an ideal location for financial markets.*

▼ *This diagram of the Bagua shows the Five Elements with their yin and yang characteristics and the directions which represent them. We can use this to arrange our workspaces to make best use of the energies of each area within them.*

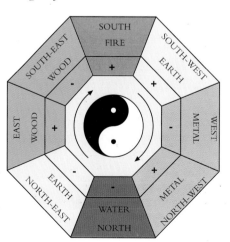

WHICH DIRECTION?

If you are setting up a new business or moving office there are considerations to be taken into account. Ideally, the entrance to an office or business should be orientated so that it faces one of the owner's best directions. Where we work for others, we should arrange our desks to face a supportive direction. We can ensure that our career is not harmed if we move jobs or buildings if we take the direction of our move into consideration.

CHOOSING A LOCATION

When relocating or setting up a new business it may be possible to choose a building with an entrance in one of our best directions. Within the building we can hopefully ensure that our desk faces one of these directions. At the very least we should attempt not to sit facing our two worst directions.

DIRECTIONS TO AVOID EACH MONTH

Every month there is a type of energy which will have a detrimental effect on

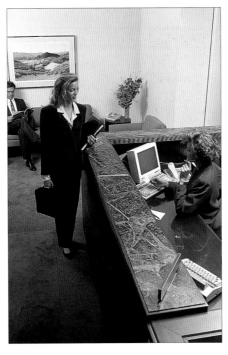

▲ *It is important to feel comfortable at work, and facing our desk in a favourable position, whatever our position in the company, helps.*

▼ *With so much competition in the financial world those who use Feng Shui in the East seem to be able to win an advantage.*

GOOD DIRECTIONS		
MAGIC NUMBER	1ST CHOICE	2ND CHOICE
1	South-east	North
2	North-east	South-west
3	South	East
4	North	South-east
5-Male	North-east	South-west
5-Female	South-west	North-east
6	West	North-west
7	North-west	West
8	South-west	North-east
9	East	South

WORST DIRECTIONS		
MAGIC NUMBER	2ND LAST	LAST
1	North-west	South-west
2	South	North
3	North-east	West
4	West	North-east
5-Male	South	North
5-Female	East	South-east
6	North	South
7	South-east	East
8	East	South-east
9	South-west	North-west

an office or business. Each month is represented by one of the twelve Chinese animals and, it is the direction ruled by the animal which sits directly opposite ours that we should try to avoid moving towards.

CHECKING THE MONTHLY DIRECTIONS

1. Locate the animal which rules the month in which you are planning to move on the "Favoured Months and Directions" diagram (opposite).

2. Locate the direction of the animal directly opposite yours. Try to avoid moving office to this direction in that month and delay the move until the following month.

FAVOURED MONTHS AND DIRECTIONS

This diagram shows the element which rules the nature of each of the 12 animals and the months and directions ruled by each.

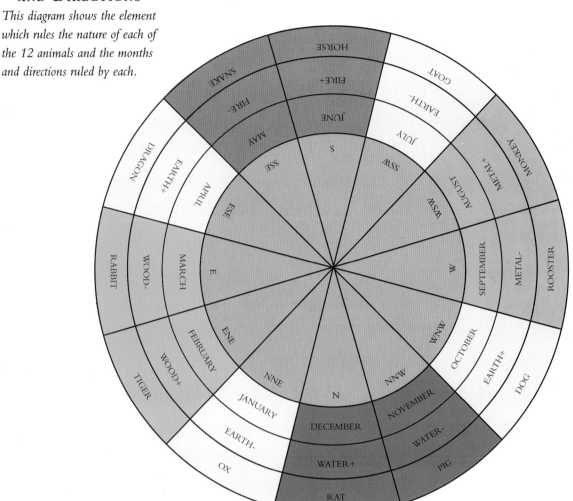

FIND YOUR FAVOURED DIRECTIONS

1. Check your Magic Number.

2. Look at the table opposite to find out the first and second choices of directions for your office to face.

YEARLY DIRECTIONS

1. Find the animal which rules the year when you are planning to move. Check the dates – the Chinese year begins in January or February.

2. Locate the direction of the animal directly opposite this animal. Avoid moving in this direction in that year.

◀▶ *When moving office, the direction the entrance faces is an important consideration.*

FIRST IMPRESSIONS

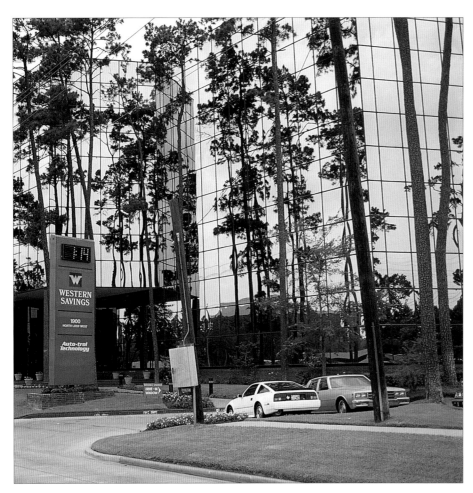

▲ *A large, clear sign, a car park and an attractive green outlook welcome visitors to this office building.*

F irst impressions of people or buildings are likely to colour our subsequent dealings with them. The ease with which we find the premises, the surrounding environment, the reception area and the greeting we receive are all indicative of the overall character and energy of a company and contribute to its success. Feng Shui can help to improve some aspects, but often it depends on the personalities involved, who will frequently determine whether we want to work with a particular organization or not.

IDENTIFICATION

On arrival at a business or office, visitors should be able to establish instantly that they have arrived in the right place. If the business occupies the whole building the company sign or logo should be prominently placed where it can be seen from the road. This may be on a signboard, but it should also be repeated on the building itself, in proportion to its size.

If the company shares a building with other businesses, a nameplate should be placed prominently outside the building and again inside to indicate which floor it is on. A notice inside the lift indicating which companies occupy each floor will make life easier for visitors, as will instructions on the wall facing the lift on each floor directing visitors to the company they are looking for or, if there is sole occupancy, to the reception desk.

COMMUNICATION

Effective communication systems are crucial to the running of a successful business. The first point of contact is usually a telephone call and this can be the first stumbling block when approaching a business.

Business cards, stationery and brochures are another point of contact which needs to be considered. Names and addresses on stationery should be clear, and if a business is in an awkward location, a small map should be included.

THE COMPANY NAME

Great importance is attached to the name of a business or retail premises. In the Chinese language, many words sound similar to others and only the intonation indicates the difference. For this reason,

▼ *A good telephone manner can make all the difference. The telephone is often the first point of contact with the company.*

BUSINESS STATIONERY

The first impression made by a letter is very important and business stationery should conform to the auspicious measurements. The colours used on the type should conform with the company colours and it is best if the name and address are in an easily readable font. The company logo should be featured and good-quality paper should be used to give a good impression.

▲ *This attractive reception area receives plenty of natural light, and drinking water is provided for staff and visitors.*

▼ *This powerful building is well signed. The name and the logo work well together and can be clearly seen.*

words which are similar to those that have undesirable meanings are not used for business names.

SIGNS

The importance of signs with a distinguishable company logo cannot be over-emphasized. Lettering should be legible. Colours are important and should be balanced according to the Five Elements. Three or five are the preferred number of colours; three representing growth and five, fulfilment. Signs along shopping malls and high streets which jut out at right angles to the building can be useful for drawing people in, especially if they are eye-catching. Signs should be firmly attached to a wall or other solid surface and should be in proportion to the whole of the building.

LOGOS

The images portrayed on a logo are important. Unpleasant and sharp images should be avoided. Points are normally not used, although an upward-pointing arrow symbolizes growth. Squares and circles are recommended, as well as images which denote upward energy. Again, colours should follow the Five Elements cycle and be balanced.

▼ *Vertical signs that jut out into the street are very eye-catching. Well-known companies will always dominate so you need to compete.*

THE WORKING OFFICE

—

How we function at work depends on a number of
factors, some within and some beyond our control.
We are usually able to organize our personal workspace
so that it supports us and enables us to work efficiently.
Other factors such as lighting, furnishings and layout
we may not be able to change ourselves, but if we do not
feel comfortable we may be able to influence the
decision-making processes in order to achieve a balanced
and harmonious environment to support us and
ultimately benefit the company.

DRAWING THE PLAN

Having determined which directions our businesses are best suited to, we can look at the internal design and layout. The various departments in an organization should be positioned in locations where the energy supports the tasks they perform.

YOU WILL NEED

◆ A compass with the eight directions clearly marked

◆ A protractor – a circular one is best

◆ A ruler

◆ A lead pencil and five coloured pencils – green, red, yellow, black/grey, dark blue

◆ A scale plan of your office space

◆ A tracing of the Bagua with the suggested information marked on it

◀ *This reception area in a restaurant enables customers to relax while they wait for their table, while being part of the atmosphere.*

TAKING A COMPASS READING

◆ Remove watches, jewellery and metal objects and stand clear of cars and metal fixtures.

◆ Stand with your back parallel to the entrance and note the exact compass reading in degrees.

◆ Note the direction faced by the entrance, in this example 95° East, and mark it on to your plan as shown in the diagram. You are now ready to transfer the compass readings on to your Bagua drawing.

TO DRAW A PLAN

Using graph paper and a tape measure, take measurements for each of the following floor-markings:

◆ External walls

◆ Internal walls

◆ Alcoves

◆ Staircases

◆ Doors

◆ Windows

◆ Permanent fixtures

This will enable you to design the final layout using the principles discussed later to position desks, furniture and other features in positions which will benefit those working there.

TRANSFER THE COMPASS READING TO THE BAGUA

1 Place the circular protractor on the Bagua diagram so that 0° is at the bottom at the North position. Mark the eight directions.

2 Find the compass reading for your office and check you have the corresponding direction. If not, you may be reading the wrong ring.

3 Mark the position of the entrance.

4 Double-check the direction, using the table opposite.

TRANSFER THE DIRECTIONS TO THE PLAN

1 Find the centre of the plan. Match the main walls across the length of the plan and crease the paper lengthways.

2 Match the main walls across the width

and crease the paper widthways. Where the folds cross each other marks the centre of your office.

If your office is not a square or rectangle, treat a protrusion less than 50% of the width as an extension to the direction. If the protrusion is more than 50% of the width, treat the remainder as a missing part of the direction.

3 Place the centre of the Bagua on the centre point of the plan and line up the entrance position.

4 Mark the eight directions on the plan and draw in the sectors.

5 Transfer the colour markings.

▼ *Once the Bagua is in place over the plan, we can see the direction of each room and the element that represents it. The location of the rooms can now be allocated.*

▲ *In a small building this reception area would probably feel oppressive. In a large office it offers the contrast of a cosy space with access to the larger space beyond.*

DIRECTIONS

North	337.5–22.5°
North-east	22.5–67.5°
East	67.5–112.5°
South-east	112.5–157.5°
South	157.5–202. 5°
South-west	202.5–247.5°
West	247.5–292.5°
North-west	292.5–337.5°

95°
EAST

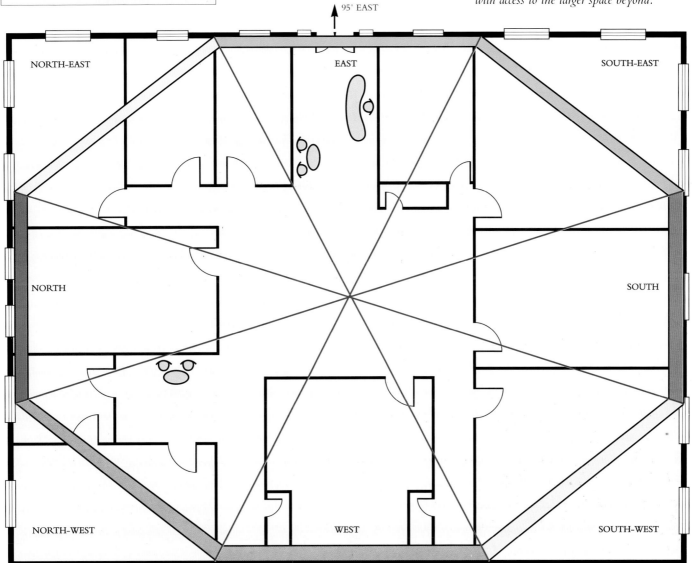

95° EAST

NORTH-EAST

EAST

SOUTH-EAST

NORTH

SOUTH

NORTH-WEST

WEST

SOUTH-WEST

DESIGNING THE LAYOUT

Taking into account the types of energy associated with each of the eight major compass directions and the types of activities suited to each, we can investigate how to design our office space accordingly. Some features – toilets, car parks and eating areas – which are more suited to some directions than others can be repositioned.

It is important to give some consideration to what visitors will see when they enter the office. Ideally, they should not be able to see directly into the main working area. Every organization has times of stress, but visitors and potential clients should not be aware of the daily traumas of office life or be able to overhear any heated conversations that may be taking place. Doors should therefore be positioned out of the line of sight of visitors, who should receive an impression of calmness and efficiency in congenial surroundings.

ENTRANCES

Entrances are auspicious if they face the favourable positions of the owner of the company, as determined by his/her Magic Number. If it isn't in our power to effect

▼ *This modern office building in Singapore is distinguished by a traditional Chinese entrance, complete with guardians on either side.*

▲ *These impressive entrance doors have been carefully designed to be in proportion to the building and its surroundings.*

▶ *A loo with a view, but the large building opposite is threatening the office with a "poison arrow" of negative energy.*

this – and usually it isn't – we can place our workstations or desks in a favourable direction instead. Entrances which face east encourage the energy of growth, while west-facing entrances foster stability. Whichever direction we face we should ensure the elements are balanced.

▲ *An attractive staff kitchen does wonders for office morale, and must be kept clean and tidy.*

BATHROOMS AND TOILETS

Always difficult to place, toilets should never face the office entrance. They should preferably be placed on an outside wall or if internally sited, ventilation must function efficiently. Bathroom doors should be closed at all times and should be

▲ *An indoor garden gives support to the fragile staircase in this light and airy reception area.*

▶ *This model office has been designed so that all the functions are in suitable directions. Work-flow has been taken into account and the doors are positioned away from public sight, while giving the widest possible view for people entering on business.*

designed so that even when open the toilets are not visible within. These areas should be kept clean and pleasant.

STAFF KITCHENS AND RESTAURANTS

Favourable areas for kitchens and restaurants are the east, south-east, south and south-west. Cleanliness and good ventilation are most important to ensure that the air is fresh and pleasant at all times.

▲ *This entrance has a lovely view but the reception desk is cut off and has beams over it.*

STAIRCASES

Ideally staircases of any kind should not be positioned in the north, north-west or the centre of the building.

CAR PARKS

Company car parks are best situated in the east, south-east and the north-west.

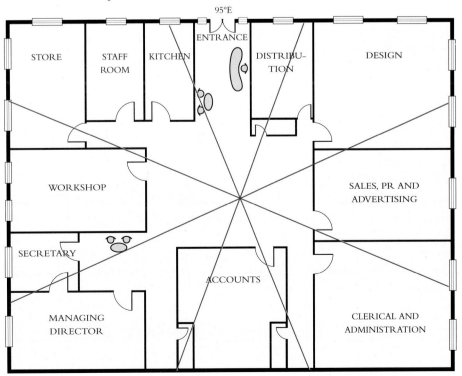

95°E

ENTRANCE

STORE | STAFF ROOM | KITCHEN | DISTRIBU-TION | DESIGN

WORKSHOP | SALES, PR AND ADVERTISING

SECRETARY | ACCOUNTS

MANAGING DIRECTOR | CLERICAL AND ADMINISTRATION

YIN AND YANG

Office activities also fall into yin and yang categories. Day-to-day administrative tasks are yin, and the yang energy is where the action is – decision-making and implementing policies. For example, a typical brainstorming session will involve several people sitting around a table in a well-lit, virtually empty room and it is almost possible to see the vibrant energy circulating around. Every now and again, a lull, a yin space, occurs when the chairman sums up the outcome before tossing another point in to build up the energy again. We can contrast this largely yang process with that of putting the ideas into practice. Programming a computer, for example, requires hours of yin time

The forces of yin and yang act together to create movement and keep a balance in the world. In the office yin and yang can relate to physical matters like layout and decor, but analysis of them also applies to the various activities which take place and to the interaction of those who work there.

Most offices tend to be more yang than yin. The straight lines of the desks, bright fluorescent lights, computer screens, shiny floor surfaces and metal cabinets, the bustle and the noise are all indicative of a yang environment. The chairman's room and the boardroom are usually remote from the hurly-burly of daily office routine and they have a more yin decor, often housing art works and other pleasing reflections of a company's wealth. In a busy office, plants can soften the harshness of the yang environment and water features can draw wealth in symbolically to the reception area, and other areas too.

▲ *This chairman's office is a yin space, decorated with paintings and with a general air of calmness.*

▼ *The straight lines and shiny surfaces of this office are yang, toned down with plants, pictures and wooden surfaces.*

▲ *This decision-making room is very functional. There are no distractions and the chairs are not too comfortable.*

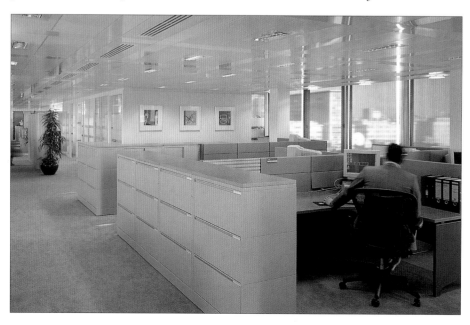

compared with an occasional frustrated outburst of yang energy when things do not go according to plan. Yin is always present within yang and vice versa.

People also fall into yin and yang categories. Some people are outwardly more dynamic and energetic, but are sometimes prone to nervous disorders and illnesses caused by physical exhaustion. However, people who proceed slowly and calmly can often surprise their colleagues by giving vent to built-up frustration. An energetic, high-powered manager may need a calm and efficient assistant, and decision-makers often need people who work in a complementary way to them to put their ideas into practice.

In an office, a balance of yin and yang is necessary for the smooth running of the organization. An office atmosphere which is too yang may mean that jobs do not get done and can result in stressful

▲ *In a hectic office the constant yang energy often results in staff becoming over-stressed.*

situations. If it is too yin productivity may be low and the company could remain static, failing to move forward and keep up with trends. As we have seen, people have either yin or yang natures and these can become evident in the workplace. Recognizing that other people work and behave differently to us is essential to a harmonious office environment.

YIN AND YANG OFFICES

YANG OFFICES CONTAIN:	YIN OFFICES CONTAIN:
Machines	Paper
Telephones and faxes	Carpets
Rectangular desks	Curtains
Blinds	Art works
Metal cabinets	Dark furniture
People traffic	One person
Conversation	Wooden cabinets
Light decor	Wallpaper
Reflective surfaces	Textured surfaces

YANG ACTIVITIES INCLUDE:	YIN ACTIVITIES INCLUDE:
Brainstorming	Administration
Deadlines	Creating
Marketing	Producing
Selling	Packaging
Promoting	Reviewing

YANG PEOPLE ARE:	YIN PEOPLE ARE:
Enthusiastic	Receptive
Energetic	Creative
Quick-thinking	Imaginative
Precise	Methodical

▶ *These two very different office spaces both show a balance of yin and yang, with straight lines and reflective surfaces softened by colours and fabrics.*

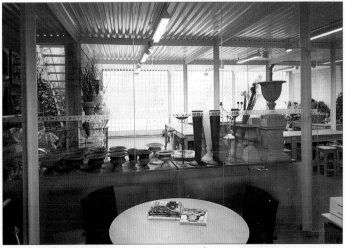

UNSEEN ENERGIES

It is now widely accepted that some buildings can create or exacerbate health problems for their occupants. Sick Building Syndrome has become a commonly accepted term for a number of problems in modern buildings which can cause minor and, occasionally, more serious illnesses or viruses. Most of these problems stem from the fact that

▲ *Office buildings with windows looking out on to green areas make better places to work.*

▼ *The air-conditioning in this office is very much in evidence, and very oppressive.*

modern buildings are virtually sealed units in which air, introduced and circulated by machines, becomes stale and a breeding ground for bacteria or viruses. This stale air is continually recirculated by air-conditioning units and the germs are constantly reintroduced to the atmosphere. A toxic mixture of chemicals from manufactured materials can also build up.

▲ *The heating and lighting systems of office blocks burn huge amounts of energy.*

THE AIR WE BREATHE
Modern buildings are designed to keep the less desirable aspects of the weather out and to regulate the temperature at what is considered to be a comfortable working level. Sealed double-glazed units

HARMFUL SUBSTANCES CAN BE FOUND IN:

FURNITURE: Particleboard, Chipboard, Plywood, Stains and varnishes, Upholstery

FURNISHINGS: Carpets, Curtains, Plastics, Paint, Wall coverings

EQUIPMENT: Photocopiers, Printers, Duplicating machines

STATIONERY: Pre-printed paper, Correction Fluids, Plastic folders, Adhesives.

▼ *We need time out from the constant pressures of modern office life to recharge our energy and also protect our health.*

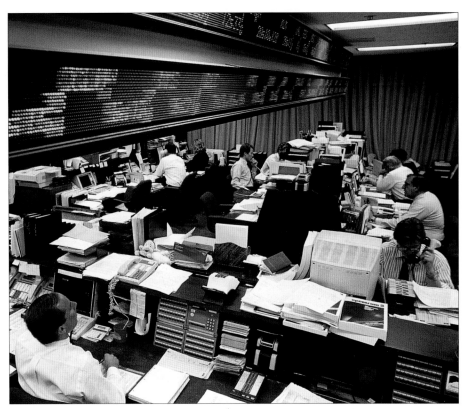

▲ *In a sealed and overcrowded office the lack of fresh air can easily cause a range of illnesses, resulting in poor productivity.*

keep out the damp and the cold, but at the same time they also prevent fresh air from circulating around a building. Some buildings have insulation in the walls which also prevents air from entering. In such buildings, air-conditioning keeps the air circulating. Dry air circulation can create throat irritation, respiratory problems, tiredness and headaches, with a resultant loss in working performance. Air that has been passed through cooling towers to add moisture to it can suffer from a build-up of bacteria and viruses in the water.

MATERIALS

Human beings function best when they are in the same range of vibrations as the Earth, which has a frequency of 8–12 hertz. Most large buildings have either steel frames or foundations made from concrete reinforced with metal rods. This metal, along with that in air-conditioning pipes and ducts, may disturb the Earth's vibrations within the building and, in consequence, have a negative effect or even harm us.

The materials which are generally used in offices are made from manufactured substances and not from natural materials. Even if the curtains are made from cotton, they are usually treated with a fire-retardant substance which releases toxic chemicals into the air. There is also an increasing incidence of allergic reactions to a variety of substances.

Where we have control over our workspaces, it is desirable to use natural materials or, if this is not possible, at least to ensure that there is a supply of fresh air. Scientists at NASA, investigating air quality inside spacecraft, discovered that some plants are useful in extracting harmful substances from the atmosphere. At the very least position one of these on your desk, especially by a computer.

PLANTS WHICH CLEAN THE AIR

Lady palm (*Rhapis excelsa*)

Dragon Tree (*Dracaena marginata*) (right)

Rubber plant (*Ficus robusta*)

Dwarf banana (*Musa cavendishii*)

Peace lily (*Spathiphyllum*)

Heart leaf philodendron

Croton (*Codiaeum variegatum pictum*)

Dumb cane (*Dieffenbachia 'Exotica compacta'*)

Golden pothos (*Epipremnum aureum*)

Boston fern (*Nephrolepis exaltata 'Bostoniensis'*)

Syngonium (*Syngonium podophyllum*) (below)

STRUCTURAL DETAILS

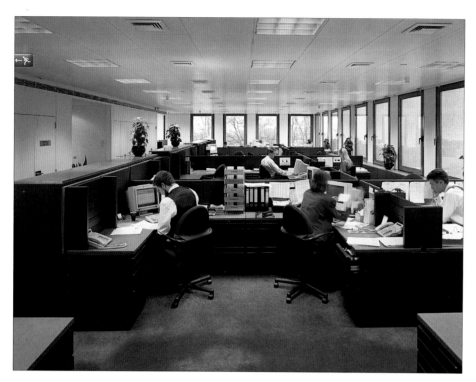

▲ The barriers between these desks do not block people sitting near to them.

Often there is little we can do about the overall structure of an office building, and we have to work with and around the layout. Old buildings with small rooms are difficult to change, but if the building is open-plan, we can introduce screens and furniture to create our own layouts. Our working conditions make a great impact on how we feel about our jobs and on our performance. Being aware of problematic features enables us to design remedies to make our working lives more comfortable.

BEAMS
Beams are not recommended in Feng Shui. They can be oppressive when positioned over a desk and can suppress the chi of those beneath them. They are necessary to support a building, and concrete beams are often a feature in offices. Desks and seating areas should not be placed underneath beams. In open-plan offices, partitions can be placed under the beams to make the best use of the space. Otherwise, filing cabinets and bookcases should be placed there, or large plants which lift the energy.

COLUMNS
Straight-sided columns are difficult to deal with. Where the edges point at chairs, the people sitting in them will feel uncomfortable. We should take measures to disguise or soften the corners of the columns by rounding them off in some way, or by disguising them with plants and other items.

BARRIERS
Where several small rooms have been converted to one large office, there are occasionally parts of walls left for structural reasons. It is important that both eyes have the same-length view, as Feng Shui consultants recognize a pattern of illnesses which result if the view from

▼ A staircase directly opposite the entrance will channel chi away from the office.

▼ The flow of chi in this room appears to have nothing to contain it.

▲ *The chi rushes straight through these wide doors and is unchecked by anything inside.*

▼ *Patterned rugs or hanging lights would slow down the energy in this long corridor.*

▼ *The giant curve slows down the movement of chi in this corridor.*

▲ *A large plant at the bottom of this light, attractive spiral staircase would give it more stability and reduce the corkscrew effect.*

one eye is blocked. Barriers can create individual workplaces, often leaving people's backs exposed. Facing another person can cause conflict, and facing the back of a computer can cause illness.

STAIRCASES

Staircases and escalators should not face the front entrance or the chi energy will be unable to circulate properly. Spiral staircases act as a corkscrew through a building and are not comfortable. Where they exist, place large plants at the bottom in terracotta pots to add stability.

CORRIDORS

Long, narrow corridors funnel chi very quickly. Slow it down by strategically placing mirrors or plants, or using other means to create a meandering route – for example, changes in floor covering or pattern. Hanging light-fittings are another option. Where there are many offices along a straight corridor, the occupants often feel isolated. If the doors are opposite one another there may be rivalry and bad feeling. A plant by each door may help and leaving doors open will enable people to feel part of the community. If doors are not aligned, this can also cause problems and it is recommended that mirrors or landscape views are placed to fill in the spaces on either side of the doors.

LIGHTING

▲ *These adaptable tilted reading stands are an ingenious way to get the light to fall on the page at the right angle.*

◀ *Natural daylight is the best source of light but in strong sunshine there is too much glare on these highly reflective glass surfaces.*

▼ *Coloured glass creates a wonderful energy in this entrance door, generating the feeling that this is a successful company.*

Adequate lighting is essential in the workplace for health and safety reasons and to ensure maximum efficiency. Offices should be well-lit and it may be necessary to introduce a variety of lighting to support the various functions which are carried out there.

NATURAL DAYLIGHT

By far the best form of lighting in an office is natural daylight. Our bodies rely on light not only to enable us to see but also for Vitamin D, which comes from the sun and is absorbed through the skin. In countries that receive relatively little sunlight during some parts of the year people may suffer from SAD, or Seasonal Affective Disorder, brought about by an excess of melatonin, a hormone produced by our brains during the hours of darkness. People who work in offices that are artificially lit will almost certainly not be as healthy as those who benefit from natural light. Depression and lethargy are typical symptoms, but working in such conditions can produce a range of problems from headaches and nausea to poor eyesight, stress and fatigue, particularly where the lighting is fluorescent.

However, precautions should be taken where computer screens and desks are close to windows since the glare of the

▲ *A range of different kinds of lighting is used in this studio. Shadows may fall in different areas at different times of day.*

▼ *In this colourful staff restaurant, elegant uplighters by the side of each table create the impression of individual spaces.*

sun can also create problems. Measures can be taken to filter the light through vertical blinds, plants or movable screens.

ARTIFICIAL LIGHT

The quality of light is important. Full-spectrum lighting was designed to copy natural daylight as much as possible but unfortunately contains slightly higher levels of ultraviolet radiation than ordinary light sources. Fluorescent lights are still the primary light source in offices because they are easy to install and cheap to run, but this type of lighting emits higher electromagnetic fields than other sources, which can be detrimental. The flickering from fluorescent lights can cause stress and headaches and can even bring on fits in epilepsy sufferers.

Incandescent light bulbs offer a range of options, giving an even light throughout the office, and can also be used for task lighting on desks. Desk lamps should always be positioned on the opposite side to the dominant hand to prevent shadows falling across work.

▲ *Interesting lighting effects enhance this attractively-designed eating area.*

Uplighters can be useful in offices where ceilings are low and where it is not desirable to have spot lighting on desks. Reflected lighting, directed on to walls and ceilings, offers an additional lighting source; the colour of the decor will influence its effectiveness. Tungsten and halogen lamps are useful for this. Too bright to be used for task lighting and close work, they give a white light which is close to daylight and the low-voltage variety can be used for accenting. These bulbs are also energy-efficient.

DECORATION

When we use colour we are working with light, as light contains all colours, each with its own frequency. The colours we use in offices will be affected by the amount of natural daylight there and by the secondary light sources we use. The materials will also have a bearing on the overall effect of the office. Upholstered chairs and curtains in dark colours have a yin quality while smooth, hard surfaces and light and metallic surfaces have yang attributes. The materials we use in decorations and furnishings have the ability to absorb or transmit light and their colours will affect the energy in the office.

COLOUR

Colour is vibration and we each respond to it consciously and unconsciously in different ways. In our own individual offices, it is best to choose wall and floor colours that we like and feel comfortable with, but in communal offices a neutral colour to suit all tastes is preferable. Colour can be introduced in furnishings and other items – paintings, storage boxes and upholstery. The psychological effects of colour are numerous but there are some Feng Shui guidelines that we can

follow. Normally offices are yang, and yang colours (red, purple, orange and bright yellow) will add to the yang energy. Yin colours (green, blue and black) will create a less dynamic feel. The colours in public areas should be neutral, with the accent colours reflecting the nature of the company, or the colours of the logo if it is one which is well-known.

▲ *Plenty of natural daylight and lively colours make this staff dining area an energetic space.*

THE FIVE ELEMENTS

The colours associated with the Five Elements evoke the quality of the energy of each element. We can use these colours in the office to highlight the

▼ *The colours of this curved reception area suggest that the company is not dependent on quick decisions or aggressive marketing.*

▼ *In this office the use of bright but muted colours and some awkward angles give the space a disturbing feeling.*

▼ *Interesting colours and shapes have been used in this design studio, where the chi moves unimpeded round the curves.*

nature of the business or the qualities we wish to invoke there.

The colours which correspond to the Five Elements should be in balance in any office. Where one element is dominant, or lacking, then it may have an effect on the energies at work there. The table below shows the relationships of the elements and can be used to strengthen a weak energy or deplete the impact of one which is too dominant. We can use the colour, shape or material related to each element to balance an environment.

If we decide to decorate our office walls in strong colours, it is usually best to choose neutral colours for furnishings or to blend the colours. However, sometimes a clash of colours is a way of moving energy, especially useful in a company where rapid decisions are called for.

MATERIALS

If we opt for a neutral colour on office walls and floors, we can introduce the qualities of the Five Elements through the furniture and fittings, soft furnishings, pictures and plants.

Hard, shiny materials, such as metal and glass, are yang and move energy on quickly. The use of these materials in staff

▲ *The green tree balances this atrium coffee bar in the centre of the building. Colourful pictures and furnishings on each level offset the white background.*

◀ *Bright Fire colours in shades of red and orange are very appropriate for a dynamic business such as this advertising agency.*

canteens and meeting rooms will ensure that the activities there do not go on too long. Denser materials such as non-shiny metals, dark wood and upholstered chairs are more containing and the energy associated with them is slower.

Synthetic materials are not really recommended because of the associated health risks and although it is inevitable that we have these materials in the office, on computer casings, furniture trims and other office items, it is preferable for them to be kept to a minimum, particularly on desks at which people spend considerable amounts of time.

THE RELATIONSHIPS OF THE FIVE ELEMENTS

ELEMENT	HELPED BY	HARMED BY	WEAKENED BY	WEAKENS
Wood	Water	Metal	Fire	Earth
Fire	Wood	Water	Earth	Metal
Earth	Fire	Wood	Metal	Water
Metal	Earth	Fire	Water	Wood
Water	Metal	Earth	Wood	Fire

ELECTRICAL EQUIPMENT

Another potential hazard in the workplace is the electromagnetic radiation from electrical equipment, particularly computers. Electromagnetic fields, or EMFs, from high-voltage power lines and electrical appliances, are thought to be injurious to health. It is believed that they impair the cell regeneration process and could be responsible for the increasing numbers of people with impaired immune systems. It is wise to sit as far as possible away from equipment and not to surround ourselves with wires. A particularly bad spot for a desk to be situated is where the mains power enters a building – desks should be moved away from that area.

▲ *Computers are an essential part of office life but it is essential to take regular breaks if our health is not to suffer.*

◄ *The impact of electromagnetic radiation on people working in this office block will be harmful.*

▼ *In such a hi-tech environment a* Cereus peruvianus *cactus might help.*

COMPUTERS

Computers are virtually indispensable in the office, yet we place ourselves at risk from a number of illnesses, ranging from eye problems to repetitive strain injury, if we spend too long in front of them. Many countries now have legislation

▼ *Wherever possible, use a laptop in preference to another computer.*

▲ *This office should be rearranged so that no-one sits behind a colleague's computer monitor.*

◄ *Shield the back of the monitor if people are sitting behind it.*

which limits the number of hours each day which can safely be spent in front of a screen. In some American states, pregnant women are not allowed to operate computers since prolonged exposure may lead to miscarriage. Screen filters help to some extent, and laptop machines do not have cathode-ray tubes which are a major cause of such problems. Wearing natural fibres also helps because they do not create static electricity.

Most of the electromagnetic radiation comes from the back of the computer monitor and when designing offices this should be taken into consideration so that no-one is sitting facing, or with their backs towards, the rear of a monitor. It is thought that some plants can help to shield us to some extent, particularly the cactus, *Cereus peruvianus*, which was adopted for that purpose by the New York Stock Exchange.

PHOTOCOPIERS AND DUPLICATING MACHINES

Photocopying and duplicating machines give off chemical emissions – the duplicating machine from the ink, and the photocopier from the toner – which are known to be carcinogenic. These machines should not be located in offices where people work all day, particularly if they are in constant use. Ideally, they should be located in a separate, well-ventilated room. Certainly, no one should sit close to a photocopier.

MOBILE PHONES

Ear and brain tumours have been attributed to the use of mobile phones. The US Food and Drug Administration advises that they should be used only when absolutely necessary and that calls should be kept short. Where it is essential to use them, ensure that the antennae do not touch the head. The use of mobile phones in cars may increase the danger, particularly hand-held models.

▼ *Mobile phones have serious health implications – use a conventional telephone whenever possible.*

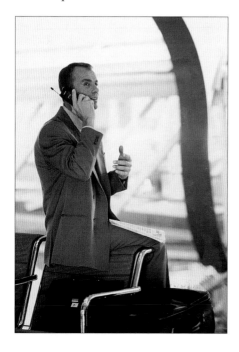

CLUTTER IN THE OFFICE

Office clutter accumulates rapidly and there are few people who would not benefit from discarding extraneous items from their workplace and streamlining their procedures. Office clutter is not just things left lying about, but also the paper we hoard, out-of-date journals and uncleared hard disks.

STORAGE

There is no excuse for clutter. There are many storage options, ranging from cupboards which hide computers and printers to simple cardboard storage boxes. These are widely available in the local high street, or by mail order. Before tidying everything away in boxes or files, it is worth asking the question, "Do I really need this?"

JOURNALS

Professional journals are invariably hoarded but rarely read. Many of these are now available on-line and professional organizations hold a complete set in their libraries if an article is needed. If we skim through journals when they arrive and note the issue and page numbers of interesting articles in a diary, we can file them.

DESKS

Desk drawers harbour a considerable amount of rubbish, but if we throw away old pens and pencils which no longer

▲ This efficient storage system is in the centre of the office, where energy should circulate freely, so it is important to keep it tidy.

work, and have special places for rubber bands and paper clips, we will feel more efficient and save time spent searching for things. It is advisable only to have a single-tier in-tray, otherwise the temptation is to categorize things into urgent and not-so-urgent, and the latter will never be dealt with. A satisfying feeling

◀ These full-length storage cupboards help to keep the office free of clutter.

▶ The top shelf of a set of shelves is rarely used and should be "weeded out" frequently.

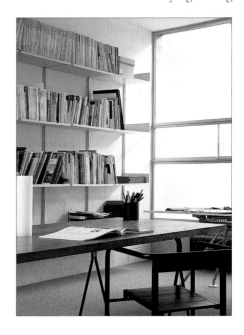

at the end of each day is to know that the in-tray is empty and that all mail has been dealt with; it can be energy-draining to begin the morning confronted with the debris from the day before. Even if you haven't been able to finish the work, tidy your desk so that you at least give the impression that all is under control. Clearing the day's mail is an excellent habit to get into and if everyone dealt with bills promptly the world would be a far less stressful place.

COMPUTERS

Computers store an amazing amount of information and if we keep the hard disks clear of out-of-date files and back up our working files regularly, we will always have rapid access to the data we need.

It can take time to set up databases to print labels for a mail shot, but it is worth the initial effort for the time saved. Random thoughts as well as notes for lectures and workshops should be recorded to help us prepare well in advance and save time and anguish at the last minute. Old hard-copy files do not have to be stored in the office and are best removed to a storeroom or cupboard elsewhere to prevent a build-up of stagnant energy.

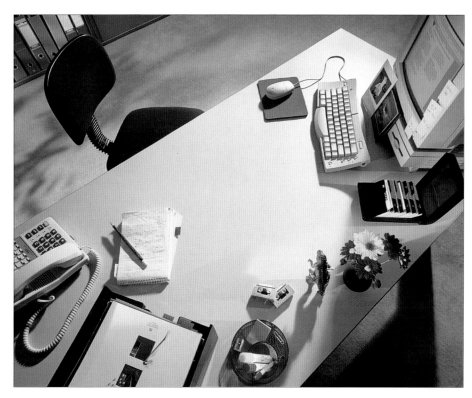

▲ *A well-organized, uncluttered desk leads to clear thinking and reduces stress.*

▼ *The storage in this reading room is good but its proportion overwhelms the table.*

ORGANIZERS

One of the most useful items in an office is a revolving card file by the telephone. Invaluable for instant access to addresses and telephone numbers, it can also be used to cross-reference suppliers, record birthdays and other information which, although it can now be stored on computers and electronic personal organizers, actually takes more time to access

in these formats. Personal organizers are extremely useful items for both the home and the office, but major difficulties arise if we lose them.

BOOKS

Many people find books difficult to discard, yet the speed of technological change renders information out-of-date rapidly and some books, such as directories and unread reference books, should be regarded as disposable items.

▼ *This well-designed workspace has both individual and communal storage areas.*

FURNITURE AND MEASUREMENTS

▲ *Floor-to-ceiling shelves overwhelm this already small office.*

◀ *This manager's office is ideally furnished but the glass panel allows no privacy.*

▲ *Furniture has to be the correct height in studios, where people bend and stretch.*

▼ *This efficient workshop has furniture at the right height and tools to hand.*

The importance of well-designed, ergonomically correct office furniture cannot be overstated. Life can become a struggle if we have to battle with stuck doors in confined spaces on a daily basis and we can cause ourselves physical harm if we sit on chairs with wobbly seats and no back support, or type on keyboards at the wrong height.

Office furniture is often neglected, particularly in offices not visited by outsiders. In small offices occupied by several people, it is important that procedures are streamlined so that storage cupboards and filing cabinets can be kept to a minimum. Positioning desks in accordance with the workflow can also help, by keeping the movement of people through the office to a minimum.

The corners of all furniture should be rounded to help movement through the office and so that the corners do not point at anyone working close by, which can be uncomfortable. Catching a hip on the corner of a desk every time we go to a cupboard, or being unable to open a door without difficulty because someone's chair is in the way, will be frustrating and may lead to tensions.

HEALTH AND SAFETY

Repetitive Strain Injury (RSI) is the result of spending a long time performing the same task and can cause great discomfort for sufferers. Wrist supports and other methods of easing the condition are available. Office managers should be sympathetic to sufferers and provide suitable furniture and equipment to alleviate the problem and to prevent it occurring in the first place.

Storage units should be at a suitable height for the items contained in them so that staff do not have to bend or stretch excessively to reach them. Shelving above head height can be oppressive and create insecurity. The edges of shelves near a chair can create "poison arrows" of energy, which can cause discomfort to those sitting nearby. Where possible, cupboards are preferable to open shelves near seating and make the office look less cluttered. Floor-to-ceiling shelving is particularly overpowering in small offices, and the more shelves we have in an office, the more likely we are to fill them up with things we do not really need. Mirrors can be placed in small offices to create an illusion of space, but do not place them where people can see themselves as they work, otherwise, depending on their personality, they will feel uncomfortable or be preening all day.

AUSPICIOUS MEASUREMENTS

(Yes = Auspicious, No = Inauspicious)

CM	INCHES	
0–5.4	0–2⅛	Yes
5.4–10.7	2⅛–4¼	No
10.7–16.1	4¼– 6⅜	No
16.1–21.5	6⅜–8½	Yes
21.5–26.9	8½–10⅝	Yes
26.9–32.2	10⅝–12¾	No
32.2–37.6	12¾–14⅞	No
37.6–43	14⅞–17	Yes
43–48.4	17–19⅛	Yes
48.4–53.7	19⅛–21¼	No
53.7–59.1	21¼–23⅜	No
59.1–64.5	23⅜–25½	Yes
64.5–69.9	25½–27⅝	Yes
69.9–75.2	27⅝–29¼	No
75.2–80.6	29¼–31⅞	No
80.6–86	31⅞–34	Yes
86–91.4	34–36⅛	Yes
91.4–96.7	36⅛–38¼	No
96.7–102.1	38¼–40⅜	No
102.1–107.5	40⅜–42½	Yes
107.5–112.9	42½–44⅝	Yes
112.9–118.2	44⅝–46¾	No
118.2–123.6	46¾–48⅞	No
123.6–129	48⅞–51	Yes
129–134.4	51–53⅛	Yes
134.4–139.7	53⅛–55¾	No
139.7–145.1	55¾–57⅜	No
145.1–150.5	57⅜–59½	Yes
150.5–155.9	59½–61⅝	Yes
155.9–161.2	61⅝–63¾	No
161.2–166.6	63¾–65⅞	No
166.6–172	65⅞–68	Yes

For dimensions in excess of these, the cycle repeats.

MEASUREMENTS

Furnishings are usually purchased from office suppliers. If they are specially designed, it will be advantageous to follow the preferred Feng Shui dimensions. It is felt in China that some dimensions bring good luck but others are not advantageous. By using the correct dimension for signs, windows, doors, desks, chairs, bookcases and other furnishings, we can ensure that we are in a strong position to develop our businesses successfully.

The measurements are taken from eight divisions of the diagonal, roughly 43 cm (17 in), bisecting a square based on the Chinese foot, which is virtually the same as an imperial foot. This

▼ *These modern chairs look attractive but do not offer enough support for the back.*

▲ *A round-edged table is ideal for meetings and prevents passers-by knocking into it.*

▼ *The manager's chair is larger than his visitor's, giving him the edge in negotiations.*

corresponds to the "Golden Section", "Divine Proportion" or pi in Eastern architecture, and is based on proportion in nature. It can be found in the growth patterns on shells and the markings on plants, among other phenomena.

The three main dimensions of office desks should be in accordance with the auspicious Feng Shui dimensions, as should the height and back width of the chairs, although the ergonomics of the furniture obviously has to conform to today's standards. Other furniture, such as bookcases and display cabinets, can also be designed according to these principles.

DESKS AND WORKSTATIONS

As we spend a considerable amount of time at work, it is important that we position ourselves where we feel comfortable and where we can tap into the beneficial energies of a supportive direction. This is easier to achieve if we are the sole occupant of an office, but

▲ *Both desks have a view of the door, with plenty of time to see someone approaching.*

▶ *Low barriers give a view of the office and do not hem people into their own space.*

even where an office is shared with other people it should be possible to find a supportive space.

The most important rule in Feng Shui is to feel comfortable and this cannot be achieved if we sit with our backs to a window or door, since we will feel uneasy and nervous. The glare of the sun through a window onto computer screens can cause headaches. A useful remedy is to place plants on the windowsill, or position a piece of furniture there, as long as this will not restrict our space.

The best place for a desk is diagonally

◀ *This desk would be better placed sideways to avoid having one's back to the window.*

opposite the door so that we can see anyone entering the room. This is certainly the place for the most senior person in the room if it is occupied by several people, as they will be bothered less by day-to-day tasks than those closer to the door. Those who sit facing the door will

DESK POSITIONS

Most of us spend a considerable amount of time at our desks so it is important to feel comfortable and well supported. This will be affected by the position of the desk in the room. Try sitting in a position that allows a view of the room while being removed from the bustle at the door, and compare it to the way you feel when you are sitting in a vulnerable position next to the door.

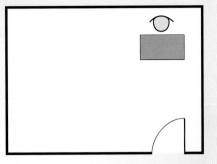

3. This position for a desk will make the occupant feel directly in the firing line.

▲ *This is a lovely desk but the chair is not supported behind. A large plant or low screen would help.*

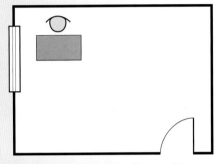

1. This is the best Feng Shui position, facing but not in front of the door.

4. This is the worst position in which one could feel comfortable.

2. This is disconcerting; some plants on the windowsill as a barrier would help.

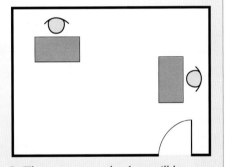

5. The person near the door will be disturbed more than the person opposite.

be in the firing line for anyone entering and those closest to it will have less job satisfaction than those further away because they will be constantly interrupted in their work by people coming in and out. People who sit in these positions rarely stay long in a job. It is their pens and equipment that visitors borrow and their papers which get knocked off the desk.

OPEN-PLAN OFFICES

In open-plan offices, desks and workstations are often in small booths and the occupants' backs face into the room. In this position, there is an element of surprise when someone approaches from behind and it is not a comfortable position in which to work. The remedy is to place a mirror on the wall.

The size of our desk should be in proportion to our position in the company. It is usual for the chairman to have a large desk and he/she would not retain much credibility if it was the smallest desk in the office.

In Feng Shui, desk shapes are important. Square and rectangular desks are considered suitable but are best if the corners are rounded so that they do not point at anyone or catch them as they

pass by. L-shaped desks are perceived to resemble meat cleavers, with the shorter side being reminiscent of the blade, which will cut off communications and authority. If possible, separate the two parts of the desk and use the smaller one for a computer. Round desks will not encourage anyone to sit and work at them for long, but are ideal for meetings, which should be kept short.

Workstations can be a problem in that they come with trailing wires. These should be secured in some way or run in channels for safety reasons. It is detrimental to health to sit facing the back of a computer monitor and every attempt should be made to design the office so that this does not occur.

▼ *Wide desks ensure that people are not sitting too close to the computer screens.*

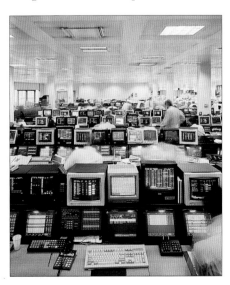

RECEPTION AREAS

The entrance to a building sets the tone for the whole company and its importance cannot be overstated. A clean, bright, welcoming entrance area will encourage clients to think well of an organization and will create a positive atmosphere for employees. A dark and scruffy area, on the other hand, will indicate a failing or shoddy company to clients and deplete the energy of employees before they start the day.

ENTRANCES

The main entrance door or doors should be in proportion to the building. If there are double doors, both should be open or the flow of chi into the building will be restricted, resulting in a dark and stale area behind the closed door. Revolving doors help to circulate energy at the entrance but are only suited to large office buildings.

Doors should open easily and not be too heavy or they will deplete personal

energy. If a company takes deliveries, or if clients bring portfolios or large sample cases, there should be some means of propping the door open to enable easy access otherwise the whole entry process will symbolize a struggle, which may continue throughout the visit. If there are windows immediately opposite the door, plants should be placed in front to prevent the chi from passing straight through without circulating around the building.

THE RECEPTION DESK

Visitors should be able to see the reception desk from the entrance but it should not be too close to it, or opposite, or the receptionist will be exhausted by the activity there. It is important that the receptionist has a comfortable chair and is backed by a solid wall so as not to be startled from behind. Receptionists should be occupied with work that will not clutter the desk and should be trained to put visitors' needs before those of

▼ *This well-designed desk enables the receptionist to keep in contact with colleagues as well as greeting clients.*

▲ *An impressive entrance, but the second door symbolizes chi escaping. It would be better turned into a window.*

▼ *This amazing sculpture is out of proportion to the entrance and exerts great pressure on it.*

▲ *The glass wall of this reception area acts as a barrier in what would otherwise have been a vulnerable position.*

◄ *The stained glass doors in this comfortable reception area add interest. Each door can be recognized by a different design.*

▼ *Care has been taken over the design of this reception area, decorated with a vase of fresh flowers.*

other employees and the demands of the telephone. Procedures should be in place to remove all deliveries from the reception area as soon as possible after arrival so that the area will not be cluttered.

RECEPTION AREAS

Chi flow in reception areas is important and employees should be able to move quickly through to their work areas via lifts and staircases. It is important that reception areas are fresh and that the air is circulated, so fans, plants and water features can play a useful role. Any water features outside the building can be reflected by mirrors in the reception area. Mirrors should be positioned to one side of the entrance so that the chi will not be reflected back through the door.

Fish tanks are often placed in reception areas. In China, fish symbolize wealth and often there are nine fish in the

tank – eight gold ones and a single black one to soak up any negative energy. Tiny darting fish create an active energy useful in commercial companies, whilst larger, slower-moving species create a calm atmosphere, which can be useful in health practices. Aquariums should be large enough to enable the fish to move freely and should recreate as natural an environment as possible.

THE IDEAL RECEPTION

This reception area contains various features to help the flow of chi:
1. A water feature with a fountain and plants lifts the chi in the reception area.
2. A well-designed reception desk supports the receptionist and is positioned so that he/she is in contact with employees and visitors.
3. Plants help to keep the air fresh and add to the Wood energy, symbolizing growth.
4. The round table indicates that energy will spin around this area quickly, suggesting that visitors will not be kept waiting long.
5. The company logo opposite the entrance adds prestige to the reception area.
6. Employees pass through this pleasant, energized area on their way to the lifts.
7. The delivery area is located close to the lifts for convenience and so that the reception area is kept clear.

COMMUNAL AREAS

◄ *Everything is incorporated in this cleverly designed office – individual spaces, meeting and eating areas, kitchen and training – and it works quite well.*

The communal areas of the office are important not just for visitors but also for staff morale. It is false economy to neglect staff areas since a contented staff that feels valued and appreciated will produce more, represent the company better and feel happier at work. Consequently there will be less absenteeism. Office and desk conditions are important but refreshment, washroom and rest room facilities are equally so.

THE ENTRANCE

Even if an office building does not have visitors on a regular basis, it is important that the entrance to the office is clearly marked and well maintained for the sake of the people who work there.

What the staff see as they arrive each day is important. Waste bins should not be placed by the entrance and deliveries should be put away immediately as they arrive. Uncollected mail and any other clutter should not be allowed to accumulate. Make sure there is someone responsible for this area. Positive images encourage staff as they arrive each day and are a "feel good" factor as they leave.

STAIRS AND CORRIDORS

Poor decoration and maintenance within the building are depressing. Shadowy corners and ill-lit passageways will not encourage staff to linger in the evening, or stay late to finish projects. Fresh paintwork and clean flooring help to create an air of efficiency and, together with

▼ *In this typical meeting room the round table encourages the circulation of ideas.*

positive images on the walls, suggest to employees that they are valued.

OFFICES

Cramped working conditions lead to cramped minds. We feel resentful if we constantly knock ourselves on colleagues' desks and cupboards. Mirrors can create an illusion of space and have a positive impact provided they do not reflect a cluttered environment. Open-plan offices can leave people feeling vulnerable so it is important that they personalize their spaces and are not surprised from behind. Strategically placed mirrors will deal with this but make sure that they are not positioned so that members of staff can see their reflections from their desk.

STAFF ROOMS

Staff rooms are where employees meet, discuss work and air grievances and the Feng Shui of these rooms is important if

▼ *A grand boardroom; the chairman sits at the head of the oval table and takes charge.*

staff are to be positive, though they should not be too comfortable or breaks will be extended. If the staff room has a kitchen area, it should be clean and conform to health and safety standards and provision should be made for clearing up at busy times. Notice boards are important and act as a communication medium between staff and employer. Notices should be up-to-date and changed regularly, and there should be a balance between work and social information.

MEETING ROOMS

Meeting rooms range from a small area where two or more people can meet to

▲ *There are only two safe spaces at this table, and all will feel very vulnerable in this glass box exposed to everyone in the office.*

▼ *This office design allows for individual workspaces and the opportunity for people to come together for discussions.*

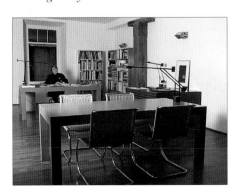

discuss a specific issue to large boardrooms. Where "Hot Desking" is practised, meetings take place standing up at hard shiny, yang tables set at "leaning height", so employees do not get too comfortable and quick decisions are made. In more conventional meetings everyone should sit facing their best direction where possible. Table shapes can affect meetings. Boardroom tables are best if they are oval. Round tables are useful for brainstorming sessions and rectangular shapes for meetings with a leader who sits at the head. Boardrooms should be well furnished and the chairperson's seat should be larger than the rest, backed by a wall with a view of the door.

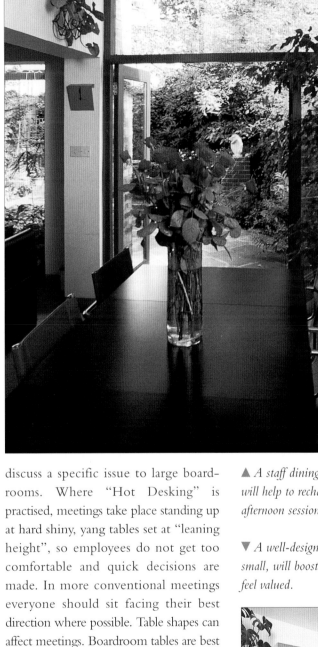

▲ *A staff dining room with a pleasant view will help to recharge energies for the afternoon session.*

▼ *A well-designed kitchen area, however small, will boost staff morale and make them feel valued.*

OFFICE ENERGIES

—

Feng Shui considers the movement of chi through a building and how it effects the working environment. It also takes into consideration the personal energies of the individuals who work there. In this section we investigate different approaches used in office communication systems, and observe how our personalities determine the way we react in certain situations, and how we respond to our colleagues. We also look at how Feng Shui can help us at interviews and on business trips, and how our home and office are linked.

OFFICE ENERGIES

THE COLLABORATIVE OFFICE

"Hot Desking" is an office design revolution that originated in architectural colleges. It is based on the idea of an open-plan office and its purpose is to encourage people to be more creative by interacting and networking in order to foster the exchange of ideas. The characteristics of this approach are:

◆ No personal space
◆ Communal desks and equipment
◆ A variety of workspaces – communal and intimate around a central hub
◆ No internal telephone calls or memos
◆ Stand-up meetings which reduces their length
◆ No departments
◆ No clutter – anything lying around is thrown out; staff have personal lockers
◆ No receptionists or secretaries
◆ All staff can do all jobs

This system has already been adopted by several companies working mainly in the area of PR and advertising. The work ethic of these types of companies is already yang and staff tend to be young and dynamic, and work under pressure.

▼ *In this typical "Hot Desking" office, the layout does not encourage people to stay long in one place.*

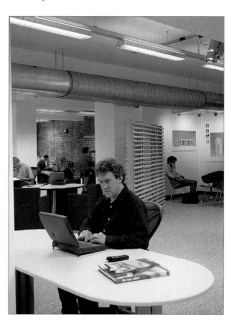

A s we have seen, Feng Shui is largely about ensuring that there is a free flow of movement around a building and arranging the space accordingly to ensure that the energy, or chi, flow does not become blocked, get stuck or stagnate. Moving furniture and redesigning space is comparatively easy and when the benefits are pointed out, there are few who cannot see the advantages, but a crucial factor that is overlooked in most organizations is the mental energy of the people who work there.

Where psychology is employed in a business, it is usually intended to bring

▲ *A happy office is a productive one. Staff need time out in a congenial space to unwind and interact with colleagues.*

advantages to the organization and to increase levels of production. While this is understandable, production will always automatically increase where staff are happy and one aspect which is generally overlooked is the fact that not everyone is the same, nor do they work in the same way. If we can accommodate a variety of working styles, then we will create a contented work force and thus generate greater productivity.

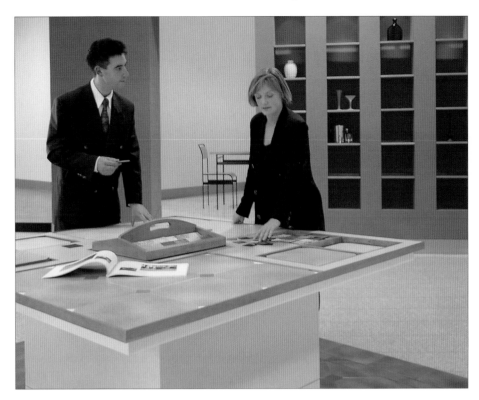

▲ *A central place for meetings and discussions ensures that ideas come from all directions.*

Such organizations need some yin in their furnishings but their efficient, clean lines suggest this is not happening, in which case the staff may feel even more pressured and eventually burn out.

At the same time as "Hot Desking" was being introduced and companies were reporting profits up by two-thirds, a report published in the *British Journal of Psychology* of a research project at Reading University suggested that open-plan offices are bad for business since their noise can affect staff, reducing their performance by 60%. It is probable that the type of people who are attracted to fast-pace media-type jobs are those who are also attracted to "Hot Desking", but it is a hard way to live for very long.

▼ *In a "Hot Desking" office different activities, such as working on a computer and discussion, are conducted side-by-side.*

THE PERSONALIZED OFFICE

Enclosed offices with no natural light will inhibit creativity, and in this type of environment, false windows, landscape pictures, mirrors and bright colours should be used to give the illusion of spaciousness. Employees should also be encouraged to make their own area a pleasant place to be in.

Marking territory lies deep in the evolutionary past of all living things. Animals scent their space to lay claim to it and repel invaders. Similarly, office workers personalize their space in some way with photographs, ornaments and other items. As a result they feel more stable and committed. Research has shown that those who do not do this tend not to stay long in any organization. A business that takes all working styles into account and provides space for different approaches and activities will have a happier, less stressed and more stable work force.

▲ *Many people in traditional offices personalize their desks with a photograph or ornament.*

▼ *A bunch of flowers is a distinctive way of making an office desk look individual as well as attractive.*

CHI FLOW

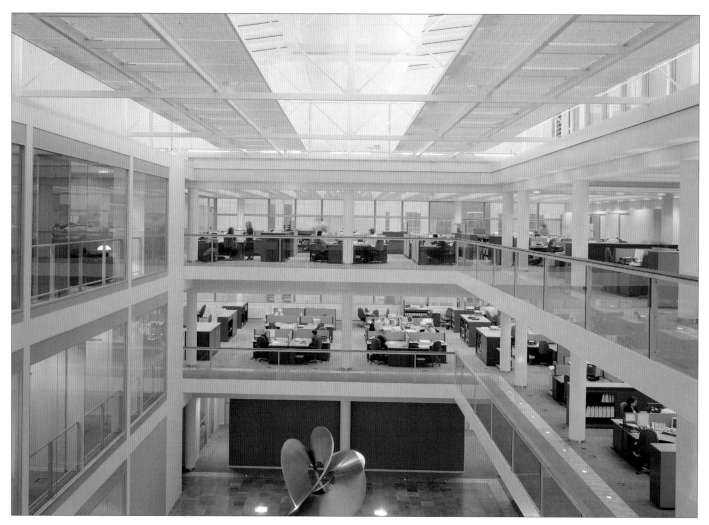

How the energy circulates in an office is important for the smooth running of the organization and also in encouraging job satisfaction and harmonious working relationships. Chi energy moves in the physical environment but its effects are subtle and affect us psychologically. Where movement, either around the building or in our dealings with colleagues, is slow or becomes stuck, this can greatly affect our performance and sense of well-being.

CHI AND POSITIONING

If we consider the model office discussed earlier in "Designing the Layout" we can see that the departments likely to import and export bulky goods are placed near the entrance. The workshops are next to the store so that products do not have to

▲ *Chi flows around each floor of these open-plan offices. The sculpture in the centre also creates energy.*

be transported through public areas and the administrative offices, accounts, sales, PR and advertising areas are all in close proximity for convenience. The managing director's office is removed from the hub of activity but is near enough to be in contact. It is linked to his/her secretary's office for speedy communication and there is a separate reception area here for important visitors, to remove them from the busy reception area.

Difficulties often arise in rooms occupied by several people and a lot of office equipment. Inevitably, some people are better positioned than others and tensions may arise. The top diagram opposite shows a badly designed office in a large

◄ *Cramming desks and people into an awkward space restricts the flow of chi.*

▲ *In this office layout the flow of chi is blocked, affecting working relationships and preventing harmony.*

▼ *The same office has been redesigned with a few simple features to give a more efficient work flow.*

organization. The occupants were irritable and visiting staff needing stationery, photocopies or advice also became irritable because the entrance was restricted and there was always a queue for the copier. If they needed stationery they had to make their way through the office and thus the occupants there had constant disruptions. The staff were often ill; the employee who sat at desk 4 suffered from headaches from the sun glaring on her computer screen as well as the fumes from the photocopier. The occupants of desks 1 and 2 faced the backs of each other's VDUs. The employee seated at desk 1 was always short-tempered as she was also in charge of the reception area and was constantly having to get up.

The next diagram shows how a few simple adjustments can make life easier and healthier. A glass screen isolated the copier, which was repositioned near the window for ventilation and reduced

congestion in the door area. All the stationery required by those not working in the office was placed near the copier so the office staff were no longer interrupted.

A reception window was cut into the wall which reduced the number of people coming into the room and the reception desk was made into a working area for the receptionist, who no longer had to keep moving from one position to another. Clutter was removed from the office and this reduced the amount of storage required, enabling the staff to have a small kitchen area with a refrigerator and a kettle. With the desks facing into the room and an empty central area, the office felt larger and less restricted and the staff were much happier.

COMMUNICATION

Day-to-day communication among staff members is of paramount importance in a successful organization. Bulletin boards in communal areas may be useful as a reinforcement, but face-to-face communication is preferable, and a short briefing meeting during the day enables staff to be informed and to air their views. These are best not held first thing in the morning. People's internal clocks vary and many take time to adjust to the working day, particularly after a bad journey. Last

▲ *Chi cannot flow properly on a narrow desk where you have to sit too close to the computer screen.*

thing in the afternoon is equally bad as staff will be anxious to get away and may already be planning the evening's activities in their minds. By around 11am most people will be settled, attentive and willing to communicate. An informed workforce which feels that its views are valued will be a productive one.

▼ *Choosing the right time of day is important if staff communication is to be meaningful for everyone concerned.*

OFFICE PERSONALITIES

We all know individuals who greet us with a smile, radiate enthusiasm for the task in hand and volunteer their services unsolicited. Conversely, there are those who never volunteer and always find a reason why an idea will not work. Personal chi, or karma, is nothing to do with Feng Shui yet it has a great impact on the office environment.

COMPATIBILITY

Our personalities are partly determined by the year in which we were born, and Chinese astrology indicates that we are compatible with some people and not others. We can use this information to maintain harmony in the workplace.

People often become unhappy at work because they are affected by the people around them. With some knowledge of the characteristics belonging to each animal sign, it is possible to arrange the workplace so that individuals working in close proximity are compatible.

STRENGTHS AND WEAKNESSES

Each of us has characteristics that lend themselves to performing certain tasks. If we can harness particular strengths and avoid placing people in areas of work which they are not suited to we can generate a happy and fulfilled workforce. The following pages describe the characteristics of each animal, and which kind of activity they do best.

▲ *An office meeting will include people of very different dispositions.*

▶ *Each coloured triangle links animals with harmonious relationships. Those immediately opposite each other are antagonistic and should be kept apart.*

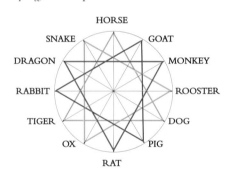

COMPATIBILITY TABLE

	RAT	OX	TIGER	RABBIT	DRAGON	SNAKE	HORSE	GOAT	MONKEY	ROOSTER	DOG	PIG
RAT	+	=	+	−	★	=	−	−	★	−	+	+
OX	=	+	−	=	+	★	−	−	+	★	−	+
TIGER	+	−	+	−	+	−	★	+	−	=	★	=
RABBIT	+	+	−	+	=	+	−	★	−	−	=	★
DRAGON	★	−	+	=	−	+	−	+	★	+	−	=
SNAKE	+	★	−	+	=	+	−	−	★	+	=	+
HORSE	−	−	★	−	=	+	−	=	+	+	★	+
GOAT	−	−	=	★	+	+	=	+	+	−	−	★
MONKEY	★	+	−	−	★	−	+	=	+	+	+	=
ROOSTER	−	★	+	−	=	★	+	=	−	+	+	+
DOG	+	−	★	=	−	=	★	−	+	+	+	+
PIG	=	+	=	★	+	−	★	−	+	+	+	−

Key: ★ Excellent   = Good   + Workable   − Difficult

THE RAT AT WORK

Rats make good bosses, team builders and leaders. Their quick minds enable them to weigh up situations at a glance and home in on important points. They do not respond well to a "nine to five" approach and work best in flexible situations.

WOOD RAT
POSITIVE: Energetic. Full of ideas. Inspirational, Popular.
NEGATIVE: Inflexible.

FIRE RAT
POSITIVE: Competitive. Flexible.
NEGATIVE: Dislikes routine. Lack of diplomacy. Low boredom threshold.

EARTH RAT
POSITIVE: Stability. Loyalty. Even temper.
NEGATIVE: Resistant to change. Intolerant.

METAL RAT
POSITIVE: High standards. Money-handling skills.
NEGATIVE: Stubborn.

WATER RAT
POSITIVE: Sociable. Shrewd. Knowledgeable.
NEGATIVE: Conservative. Indiscreet.

THE OX AT WORK

Loyal, hardworking and honest, Oxen systematically undertake any task, often working beyond the call of duty to complete it. They do not easily tolerate what they perceive to be slacking in others.

THE TIGER AT WORK

Tigers are dynamic and can carry others along by sheer enthusiasm. They are always very eager to launch themselves into new ventures. On the other hand, they often make rash decisions and can be very critical of the others. They enjoy a challenge and have good leadership skills.

WOOD OX
POSITIVE: Leader. Spokesperson. Confident. Hard-working.
NEGATIVE: Quick-tempered

FIRE OX
POSITIVE: Determined. Honest. Protects staff. Perceptive.
NEGATIVE: Outspoken. Inconsiderate.

EARTH OX
POSITIVE: Loyal. Accurate. Shrewd.
NEGATIVE: Slow. Uninspiring.

METAL OX
POSITIVE: Energetic. Reliable.
NEGATIVE: Outspoken. Selfish.

WATER OX
POSITIVE: Integrity. Persistent. Respects the views of others.
NEGATIVE: Sensitive.

WOOD TIGER
POSITIVE: Team player. Positive. Tolerant. Innovative.
NEGATIVE: Short attention span. Aloof. Temper. Ego.

FIRE TIGER
POSITIVE: Popular. Resourceful. Optimistic.
NEGATIVE: Restless. Loner.

EARTH TIGER
POSITIVE: Analytical. Practical. Objective.
NEGATIVE: Lacks humour. Insensitive. Pushy.

METAL TIGER
POSITIVE: Assertive. Competitive. Risk taker. Staying Power.
NEGATIVE: Aggressive. Headstrong. Self-centred.

WATER TIGER
POSITIVE: Intuitive. Objective. Understanding.
NEGATIVE: Vengeful. Procrastinator.

THE RABBIT AT WORK

Rabbits are polite, considerate and dislike conflict of any sort. They wilt under criticism and dislike being backed into a corner and will always find a means of escape. Flexible, they refuse to panic. Artistic and intuitive, rabbits never miss anything. They keep close counsel and advance by weighing up situations and methodically taking advantage of them until they achieve their goals, often to the surprise of others. Rabbits have strong wills and an inbuilt sense of self worth.

WOOD RABBIT
POSITIVE: Generous. Accommodating. Flexible.
NEGATIVE: Indecisive. Lenient. Impersonal. Vain.

FIRE RABBIT
POSITIVE: Fun-loving. Progressive. Intuitive. Diplomatic.
NEGATIVE: Temperamental. Outspoken. Neurotic.

EARTH RABBIT
POSITIVE: Persistent. Trustworthy. Rational. Prudent.
NEGATIVE: Calculating. Materialistic. Introverted.

METAL RABBIT:
POSITIVE: Intuitive. Dedicated. Thorough. Ambitious.
NEGATIVE: Moody. Cunning. Intolerant.

WATER RABBIT
POSITIVE: Supportive. Good memory. Friendly.
NEGATIVE: Over-sensitive. Emotional. Indecisive.

THE DRAGON AT WORK

Dragons are entrepreneurs and leaders. They have an irrepressible energy and an unswerving confidence in their abilities. Dragons find it difficult to keep secrets and will not accept criticism, and a crossed dragon is a sight to behold.

WOOD DRAGON

POSITIVE: Innovative. Generous.
NEGATIVE: Proud. Condescending.
Outspoken. Pushy.

FIRE DRAGON

POSITIVE: Objective. Competitive.
Inspirational. Enthusiastic
NEGATIVE: Demanding. Inconsiderate.
Aggressive. Impetuous.

METAL DRAGON

POSITIVE: Honest. Charismatic.
NEGATIVE: Intolerant. Inflexible.
Ruthless. Critical.

WATER DRAGON

POSITIVE: Methodical. Resourceful.
NEGATIVE: Autocratic. Impersonal.
Pragmatic.

EARTH DRAGON

POSITIVE: Sociable. Fair. Initiator.
NEGATIVE: Bossy. Distant.

WOOD SNAKE

POSITIVE: Intuitive. Far-sighted.
Logical. Staying power.
NEGATIVE: Vain. Aloof. Big spender.

FIRE SNAKE

POSITIVE: Confident. Perseverance.
Charismatic. Ambitious.
NEGATIVE: Self-centred. Suspicious.
Jealous. Uncompromising.

EARTH SNAKE

POSITIVE: Trusting. Calm. Reliable.
Shrewd.
NEGATIVE: Conservative. Frugal.

METAL SNAKE

POSITIVE: Generous. Co-operative.
Self-sufficient. Opportunistic.
NEGATIVE: Suspicious. Scheming.
Uncommunicative. Domineering.

WATER SNAKE

POSITIVE: Intuitive. Practical.
Organized. Determined.
NEGATIVE: Secretive. Vindictive.
Calculating.

THE SNAKE AT WORK

 Snakes have an inner wisdom which, combined with intelligence, make them formidable. They usually follow their own path and leave the mundane tasks to others. If attacked they find subtle ways of revenge. Snakes are intuitive and are not easily fooled; they have a dry sense of humour.

THE HORSE AT WORK

 Horses have low boredom thresholds and attention spans. They like action and short, to-the-point instructions. Capable of work-ing tirelessly to meet a deadline, they adhere to their own timetables and like flexibility. They are perceptive and have lightning brains and can come to conclusions in an instant, although they may occasionally come to the wrong one. They work on hunches and are great improvisers. Their tempers are quick to flash, but they soon forget the cause.

WOOD HORSE

POSITIVE: Logical. Inspirational.
Intelligent. Friendly.
NEGATIVE: Restless. Highly strung.
Lacks discernment.

FIRE HORSE

POSITIVE: Intellectual. Flamboyant.
Passionate.
NEGATIVE: Volatile. Troublesome.
Inconsistent.

EARTH HORSE

POSITIVE: Methodical. Adaptable.
Logical. Amiable.
NEGATIVE: Indecisive. Overstretches.

METAL HORSE

POSITIVE: Intellectual. Intuitive.
Logical. Enthusiastic.
NEGATIVE: Headstrong. Unfinished
tasks. Foolhardy.

WATER HORSE

POSITIVE: Adaptable. Spontaneous.
Cheerful. Energetic.
NEGATIVE: Indecisive. Inconsiderate.

WOOD GOAT

POSITIVE: Compassionate. Peace-loving. Trusting. Helpful.
NEGATIVE: Clinging. Resistant to change.

FIRE GOAT

POSITIVE: Courageous. Intuitive.
Understanding.
NEGATIVE: Spendthrift. Volatile.
Impatient.

EARTH GOAT

POSITIVE: Sociable. Caring.
Optimistic. Industrious.
NEGATIVE: Sensitive. Conservative.
Self-indulgent.

METAL GOAT

POSITIVE: Artistic. Adventurous.
Self-confident.
NEGATIVE: Possessive. Moody.
Vulnerable.

WATER GOAT

POSITIVE: Articulate. Friendly.
Popular. Opportunistic.
NEGATIVE: Silky. Dislikes change.
Impressionable. Emotional.

THE GOAT AT WORK

 Goats get on well with everyone. They cannot bear confrontation and wither when disciplined. Schedules and dead-lines are not for Goats, who thrive when allowed complete freedom. Goats are idealistic and often impractical and yet they usually seem to bring others to their way of thinking by their charm and persistence. When it doesn't happen, they will sulk. Survivors, Goats worry a lot and need approval to function effectively.

THE MONKEY AT WORK

 Naturally sociable, the monkey will always have a following. His quick wit and leadership skills ensure he is never isolated. Monkeys are capable of great achievement and know it. They do not suffer from false modesty, neither do they

WOOD MONKEY

POSITIVE: Intuitive. Resourceful. Persistent. Inventive.
NEGATIVE: Restless. Dissatisfied. Rash.

FIRE MONKEY

POSITIVE: Self-confident. Truthful. Self-motivating.
NEGATIVE: Domineering. Mistrustful. Jealous. Confrontational.

EARTH MONKEY

POSITIVE: Reliable. Generous. Scholarly. Honest.
NEGATIVE: Moody. Rude. Unlawful.

METAL MONKEY

POSITIVE: Self-reliant. Loving. Creative. Hard-working.
NEGATIVE: Proud. Uncommunicative. Inflexible.

WATER MONKEY

POSITIVE: Kind. Flexible. Persuasive.
NEGATIVE: Touchy. Secretive. Evasive.

WOOD ROOSTER

POSITIVE: Enthusiastic. Reliable.
NEGATIVE: Easily confused. Regimental. Blunt

FIRE ROOSTER

POSITIVE: Independent. Organized. Dynamic.
NEGATIVE: Fanatical. Inflexible. Temperamental.

EARTH ROOSTER

POSITIVE: Hard-working. Efficient. Careful.
NEGATIVE: Critical. Dogmatic.

METAL ROOSTER

POSITIVE: Industrious. Reforming.
NEGATIVE: Opinionated. Uncompromising. Inhibited.

WATER ROOSTER

POSITIVE: Persuasive. Energetic. Practical.
NEGATIVE: Fussy. Bureaucratic.

boast. Monkeys are problem-solvers. Entirely flexible, they manipulate situations to achieve their goals. They learn quickly and their fine memories mean that no one gets the better of them. On the rare occasion that this happens, monkeys will bounce back.

THE ROOSTER AT WORK

Roosters are proud and opinionated and are prone to offering unsolicited advice. They are however, on their good days, outgoing and amusing and make good company. They never miss anything and are real sticklers for detail, Roosters exel at accounts and will not miss even the smallest error. If the mistake is yours you will never hear the end of it.

THE DOG AT WORK

Dogs are sociable and fair, they are also reliable. If there is a cause to fight for, or if someone they know needs some help and support, the Dog will be there. Dogs

WOOD DOG

POSITIVE: Likeable. Calm. Honest.
NEGATIVE: Hesitant. Ingratiating.

FIRE DOG

POSITIVE: Leader. Innovator. Honest.
NEGATIVE: Rebellious. Strong-tempered.

EARTH DOG

POSITIVE: Fair. Efficient. Stable. Kind-hearted.
NEGATIVE: Secretive. Demanding. Show-off.

METAL DOG

POSITIVE: Dedicated. Decisive. Charitable.
NEGATIVE: Secretive. Demanding. Extreme.

WATER DOG

POSITIVE: Sympathetic. Fair. Calm. Democratic.
NEGATIVE: Distant. Indulgent.

WOOD PIG

POSITIVE: Organising. Promoter. Orator.
NEGATIVE: Manipulating. Gullible.

FIRE PIG

POSITIVE: Optimistic. Risk taker. Determined.
NEGATIVE: Bullying. Underhand.

EARTH PIG

POSITIVE: Patient. Reliable. Diligent.
NEGATIVE: Unyielding.

METAL PIG

POSITIVE: Sociable. Direct. Enduring.
NEGATIVE: Domineering. Tactless. Resentful.

WATER PIG

POSITIVE: Persevering. Diplomatic. Honest.
NEGATIVE: Over-indulgent. Slapdash. Gullible.

work well with those they like but can ignore or dismiss those they don't get on with. If crossed, their tempers are quick, though they do not bear grudges. They will reluctantly accept, but are not really happy in, the limelight. Dogs keep a clear head in a crisis and inspire confidence in others. Their preference for a quiet life can give the impression of moodiness.

THE PIG AT WORK

Pigs are the stabilizing force in an office. Amiable and always willing, pigs rarely attract dissent, although they can waste time in pursuing unlikely schemes. Pigs are never crafty and have an endearing innocence which attracts others to them. Competitive is not a word known to pigs who may occasionally be ridiculed for their slow reactions. Pigs are responsible and accurate workers. If there are any problems, pigs will take up the cause and carry others with them. Rarely do they flare up but when they do it will only be fleeting, then all will be forgotten.

HOME-OFFICE LINKS AND THE BAGUA

When there are problems with no obvious cause in the home, a Feng Shui consultant will often look to the office, and vice versa. However good the Feng Shui of the home and the office, karma is paramount, as of course is destiny. There are steps that can be taken to improve life, even where the odds appear to be stacked against us. Healthy lifestyles and positive attitudes help and Feng Shui can tip the balance.

A POSITIVE ATTITUDE

Negative attitudes are self-destructive and a sure way of provoking a negative reaction from others. Negative people are far less likely to get a contract or promotion than those who are always willing to try something and appear enthusiastic. Being positive is easier if we are fit and healthy and if our lives outside the office environment are happy and fulfilled. Using Feng Shui is just part of the package that will enable us to achieve what we want in life. If we live in a chemical and electromagnetic soup, eat food that is contaminated by chemicals and spend our leisure time slouched behind closed curtains in front of a TV screen, we will

▼ *We should only use the Bagua for ourselves. It would be difficult to use on this shared desk without affecting other people.*

▲ *Supple, healthy bodies enable the chi to flow unobstructed through them.*

◄ *If we spend our days like this, then our leisure activities should offer exercise and time away from electrical equipment.*

not be as healthy or able to cope with our increasingly complex society as someone who eats fresh food, exercises the body and the mind and is open to a wide range of people and experiences.

SLEEP AND HEALTH

We can use Feng Shui to make sure we are sleeping in a direction that supports us. The best direction – the one in which it is best to site our doors, desks and beds – is the one to use if all is well. There is another direction, known as the Celestial Doctor, which is useful if we are ill. It is used to tap into the energies of the universe and aid recovery. Refer to the table to the right.

USING THE BAGUA

The Bagua is a tool we can use to focus on various aspects of our lives. We can

align it to the compass directions and position it on a plan of our homes and offices, or on our desks. We can also use it to represent a symbolic journey of our lives by aligning it to where we sit at our

BED DIRECTIONS

MAGIC NUMBER	BEST DIRECTION	CELESTIAL DOCTOR
1	South-east	East
2	North-east	West
3	South	North
4	North	South
5 (Male)	North-east	West
5 (Female)	South-west	North-west
6	West	North-east
7	North-west	South-west
8	South-west	North-west
9	East	South-east

(NB: These are the directions of the bedroom in the house and are also to be faced by the top of the head when lying down.)

desks or to the front of our houses. Most people want to focus on two areas – the Career path and Wealth. Equally as important are the Helpful People who will make success possible.

THE CAREER AREA

This area represents the start of our journey. It sits in the north direction, represented by the Water element. A water feature here will support the energy of the area and Metal will give it a boost so a wind chime or other metal object here would be helpful. A black-and-white picture representing both Water and Metal would also be useful. If we are using the Bagua symbolically, we will need to check that anything we place will not clash with the elemental energy there. We may prefer to use a brochure of the organization we wish to gain employment in or the business card of the company whose account we are hoping to take on. We can enhance the Career area in our homes, but we would need to have a private office to do this at work or we will be taking responsibility for the careers of colleagues as well.

THE HELPFUL PEOPLE AREA

By stimulating the Helpful People areas in our homes or in our offices, we

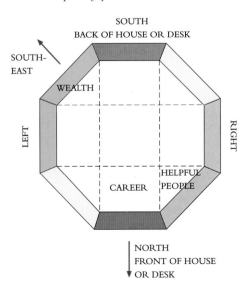

▼ *The Bagua can be positioned on to your workstation or desk, just as you would place it over a plan of your house.*

▲ *Using the principles of Feng Shui in the home will have the combined effect of improving life at work; the two worlds are inextricably linked.*

encourage the support of others. This is a Metal area and Metal is supported by Earth. Therefore a rock, terracotta pot or crystal here will stimulate the energy. Again, if using the Bagua symbolically, the element of the direction should be checked and the elements should be balanced. Be careful when hanging crystals; anything harmful reflected in them will be magnified by their many faces and break up rather than encourage beneficial energies.

WEALTH

Many people are attracted to Feng Shui by the promise of wealth, as represented by the Wealth corner of the Bagua. If only it were that simple! We have seen that Feng Shui is only part of the picture

and that other forces such as destiny and personality come into play. If there is no demand for your services, Feng Shui cannot help. The Wealth area is a Wood area and a plant will support the energy. Other options are an empty pot placed ready for the wealth to pour in, some coins in a dish or a bowl of spring water that has been placed in moonlight and is changed every day.

▼ *We can align the Bagua to our desks and activate an area. This desk is well organized but cluttered. A small trolley to hold equipment would be useful.*

INTERVIEWS

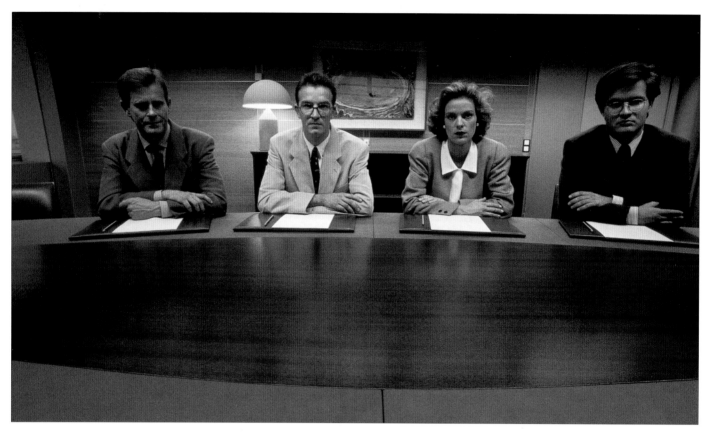

Interviews are often gruelling and many factors besides professional competence play a part in the selection procedure. There is nothing we can do about our compatibility with members of the selection panel, but we can make use of some Feng Shui techniques to give us the best possible chance of acquiring a job. Other factors which will play a part are punctuality, awareness of the impact of our body language and maintaining eye contact.

▼ *Gestures and facial expressions tell us a lot about other people.*

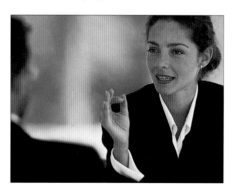

CLOTHES

Research has shown that given the choice of three women candidates, one in a business suit, one in a suit but with the addition of a scarf or a piece of jewellery, and one in floral dress, most interviewers opt for the candidate in the business suit (a yang outfit) with some (yin) additions on the grounds that it looks professional but not as if the woman is trying to emulate a man. Obviously it is not always necessary to wear such an outfit and a business suit might even be inappropriate in some areas of employment. Feng Shui can help by suggesting which colours suit us and the jobs we are seeking so that we can use them either in accessories or in the outfit we wear. This does not just apply to women; men can use their suitable colours in ties, shirt patterns and socks.

Women in a predominantly male profession may feel more confident if they introduce some yang colours into their clothing – reds, purples and oranges. If a

▲ *Faced with a panel like this, you can at least move your chair to face a good direction.*

▼ *Body language plays an important part in communicating with other people.*

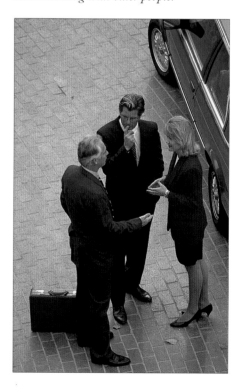

man wishes to be employed in an occupation that is usually the domain of females, then some yin colours – blues and greens – will be appropriate.

Each of the Five Elements is associated with different types of professions. It may be useful to introduce something of the energy of the business into clothing or even into any files or pens we carry to the interview. The table below indicates the elements associated with some of the most common businesses.

WHICH DIRECTION

Sometimes we will have the opportunity to choose where to sit. Many large organizations' selection processes now

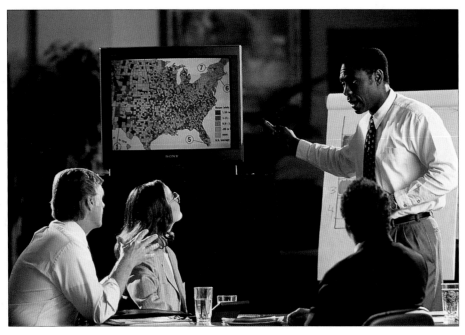

▼ Each of the Five Elements is particularly relevant to different types of business. These are some of the most common.

▲ If you need to give a presentation, it is important to face a direction that is auspicious for you.

require candidates to mingle and dine with executives prior to formal interviews. If we take a small compass with us and familiarize ourselves with the orientation of the building, we may be able to sit in our best direction. If we have to give a presentation, we should aim to orientate ourselves to face one of our best directions. Even during a formal interview, it may be possible to move the chair slightly so we can gain the advantage of facing an auspicious direction. The table below is a reminder of our best direction based on our magic numbers.

WOOD	FIRE	METAL	EARTH	WATER
Green/Jade	*Red/Purple*	*White/Grey*	*Yellow/Brown*	*Dark Blue/Black*
Horticulture	Marketing	Accountancy	Agriculture	Communication
Floristry	PR	Banking	Building	Electrical
Forestry	Advertising	Mining	Food	Fishing
Wood crafts	Fashion	Jewellery	Pottery	Transport
Publishing	Law	Engineering	Personnel	Travel
Media	Chemicals	Appliances	Clothing	Health

◄ In an interview, Feng Shui can give us that "extra something".

▼ When you go into an interview, always remember your best direction.

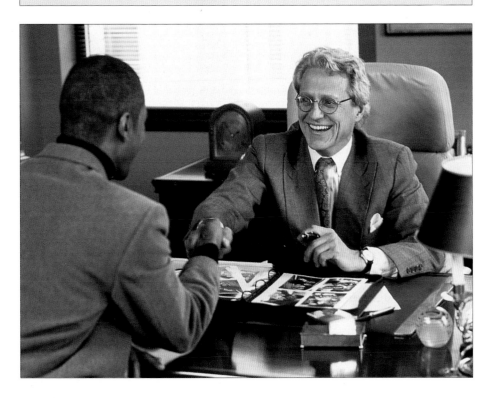

MAGIC NUMBER	
1	South-east
2	North-east
3	South
4	North
5 (Male)	North-east
5 (Female)	South-west
6	West
7	North-west
8	South-west
9	East

BUSINESS TRIPS

We should follow the same procedures on business trips as we do in our homes and offices. If the trip is important and much rests on the outcome, then it is worth requesting a room in one of our best directions when we book the hotel. When packing for a business trip, always remember the compass. This will enable us to position ourselves in an auspicious direction when we are negotiating, and to align our beds to beneficial energies as we sleep.

TRAVEL ARRANGEMENTS

The energy of certain months suggests that we should not move towards a certain direction. In the "Favoured Months and Directions" diagram, we can see which of the twelve Chinese animals rules each month. It is inadvisable to move towards the direction opposite the animal which rules each month, during that month. For example, in November, which is ruled by the Pig, it would not be wise to travel in the south–south-east direction. Travelling in this direction may have result in misunderstandings and the

▼ *If you are in charge of a group, keep their instructions clear and precise.*

break-up of negotiations. Although the indications are that this will only be of a temporary nature, it is obviously best to try and avoid such complications. If it is possible to alter the route of your journey so that you travel towards your destination from another direction, this will reduce the impact.

THE MEETING

Whether we meet clients or colleagues in a public place or in their offices, we can attempt to gain some advantage for ourselves if we pay attention to where we sit. We should always try to be supported by a wall behind us and never sit with our backs to a door, or at a window. In addition, if we can manoeuvre ourselves so that we face our best direction then we will be in an advantageous position.

THE HOTEL ROOM

It will benefit us if our head faces one of our auspicious directions as we sleep. The position of the bed is important and we should attempt to ensure that we are supported by a wall behind and that we do not face the ensuite bathroom since negative energy will emanate from it. If the bed does face the bathroom, make sure

▲ *Business trips can be tiring and frustrating. It helps if you can arrange to travel in an auspicious direction.*

▼ *Laptops enable us to make use of travelling time. If possible, place them so that you face an auspicious direction.*

PACKING TIPS

A compass
Details of your best directions
Something to cover a mirror
Incense or oils and a burner
A water spray
The name of a good restaurant to
    celebrate success

▲ *When you want to dominate, choose the prime position for yourself and the vulnerable one for your client.*

that the door is closed at all times. A mirror facing the bed is not considered to be good Feng Shui and we will have a disturbed sleep if we do not cover it. Many hotel beds are surrounded by electrical cables for bedside lamps, telephones and radios. Some are even built into the headboard and there is little we can do about them. Switch off and unplug all appliances and move the bed away from them if possible.

Hotel rooms will have accumulated the chi energy from all those who have been there before us. It is obviously better for us if we can remove this energy and create a pleasant environment for ourselves. Opening windows to let in fresh air is an obvious starting point. It may be difficult, because of the noise involved, to raise the sound vibrations in the room by clapping, ringing bells and

▲▼ *Unplug electrical appliances before you fall asleep. Cover a mirror or television screen as they will both reflect the bed.*

making other noises to perk up the energy, but we can silently improve the air quality by burning incense or aromatic oils and spraying water around the room to increase the negative ions.

Having created as much of a temporary home-from-home for ourselves as is possible, and tapped into our beneficial energies, we should place ourselves in the most advantageous position possible for our business discussions.

ENTERTAINING

When we take clients out to a restaurant, we can place ourselves in suitable positions to make the negotiation process work to our advantage. We can ensure that those we wish to score points against are placed in a vulnerable position – for example, with their backs to the door or in the path of cutting chi from the corner of a pillar. If, on the other hand, we want to win someone over, it may be worth allowing them the supported position while we sit in our best direction.

FENG SHUI AND YOUR CAR

▲ *Our cars, just like ourselves, need to be kept healthy and in good condition.*

Many people spend hours at a time in their cars which become like mini-homes. Like our homes, they become a reflection and extension of ourselves. Negative chi in cars has the power to create lasting damage and destruction to their owners and to others. Cars are extensions of ourselves. With the right treatment they serve us well. Some people talk to their cars, others give them names and personalize them. In some parts of the world they are blessed. Negative energy breeds negative response, so we should aim to build up a caring relationship with our cars.

Generally, cars follow the classic Four Animals formation, being taller at the back than the front, and having support on either side. Car seats should also follow this formation. Cars which slope away to the back and those which open at the back can leave us feeling insecure, as anyone who has driven off as a rear

▼ *Yellow, an Earth colour, representing stability, is auspicious.*

door or boot (trunk) lid has flown open can testify. Small pick-up trucks are vulnerable from behind since their cargoes can fall off or may be stolen.

The rear lights act as our Tortoise, warning those behind to brake. It is therefore essential to ensure they are clean and in working order, and that spent bulbs are replaced immediately. Cars with reclining seats, such as expensive sports models, also suggest vulnerability behind since the Tortoise position is weak. Their "laid-back" effect is often reflected in the driving habits of the owners of such cars.

CAR ORNAMENTS

Stickers on the rear window can strengthen the Tortoise position, particularly those which say "Please Keep Your Distance" or "Baby on Board" and other, polite, warning signs. Jokes and stickers which are difficult to read have the opposite effect in that they encourage the car behind to come closer. Stickers should not obstruct the window.

Any ornaments that act as a distraction behind should be avoided. The windscreen can act as the Phoenix and moving objects, like hanging ornaments, can create instability and affect concentration. Do not allow loose items to collect in the

▲ *The white Metal energy drains the flamboyant red on this quirky car.*

back of the car as sudden braking will send them cannoning around.

Even people who would not admit to being superstitious carry talismen when they travel. In the West, a small St Christopher symbol is believed to be protective because he was the patron saint of travellers. Other cultures have their own protection symbols. Attitudes to numbers on registration plates also indicate cultural differences. The Chinese avoid 4 because it resembles the word for death, while Westerners prefer not to use 13 and treble 6 for superstitious reasons.

▼ *Our cars reflect our personalities. An untidy car is as revealing as an untidy home. Secure anything that rattles.*

THE CAR AND THE SENSES

Fresh air is necessary in cars, in order to link the occupants with the world outside and to cleanse the air within the confined space. If the air is not fresh, the driver can become tired and lose concentration. To freshen the air we can introduce natural oils, which also affect our moods. Rosemary, neroli and lemon oils are helpful for calming anger and promoting clear thinking.

Vision is important in the car and a clean screen and headlights enable us to see and be seen clearly on a foggy day and at night.

If we regard the car engine in the same way that we do our bodies, then we

ELEMENT	HELPED BY	HARMED BY	WEAKENED BY	WEAKENS
Wood	Water	Metal	Fire	Earth
Fire	Wood	Water	Earth	Metal
Earth	Fire	Wood	Metal	Water
Metal	Earth	Fire	Water	Wood
Water	Metal	Earth	Wood	Fire

can appreciate that for the car to be healthy and function well its tubes have to be unblocked and its components well maintained. Regular servicing is therefore important.

PERSONALITY AND THE CAR

Our cars reflect our personalities in the same way as our homes do. A neat, clean car generates a different impression of its owner to a dirty one. The colours we choose also affect our attitude to a car and the perception other drivers have of us. How many of us give red cars driven by very young men a wide berth? When choosing cars we would do well to bear the Five Elements relationships in mind.

CHOOSING THE COLOURS

We should ensure the colours of our cars do not conflict with the colour of the element associated with our Chinese animal. For example, a young and rather macho male, particularly a Fire Horse,

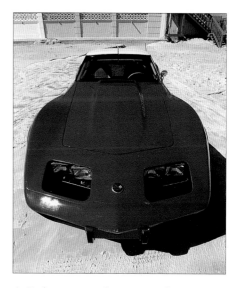

▲ *Red sports cars show too much yang. Black accessories will reduce the impact.*

should not choose red because this colour will intensify the fire. A dark blue or black to cool the Fire, and Metal – white or grey – to weaken it is preferable, and safer. On the other hand, a driver who cannot concentrate and who is a Water Pig will need some Wood (green) to draw them on and some Metal, white or silver, as support.

CAR CLUTTER

Rattles left unfixed

A worn spare tyre

Spent lamps

Confectionery wrappers

Fast-food cartons

Car park tickets

Rubbish in the boot (trunk)

▼ *Young male energy is excessively yang. Black, a yin Water energy, will drain it.*

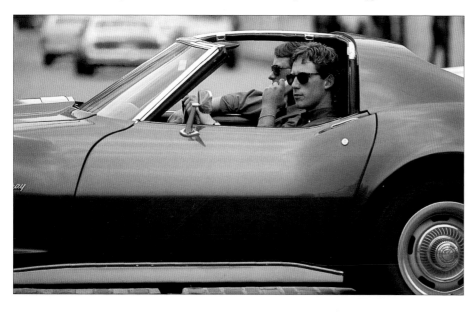

CAR NUMBERS

Number associations vary between different cultures. In China, they often depend on sound. The number 4 sounds like the Chinese word for 'death' and is therefore considered unlucky. The number 8 on the other hand sounds like the Chinese word for "happiness" and is well-regarded. 88 is therefore doubly auspicious, meaning "double happiness". Car number plates containing the number 888 are very sought-after and command high prices.

PICTURE ACKNOWLEDGEMENTS

The publishers would like to thank the following picture libraries for the use of their pictures.

Houses and Interiors: 87tr(Mark Bolton).

Hutchinson Library: 8br(Robert Francis); 10tr(Merilyn Thorold); 13tr(Melanie Friend); 26bl(T. Moser), br(Lesley Nelson); 27tl(F. Horner); 28t(Edward Parker), bl(Sarah Errington), r(John G .Egan); 29bl(Tony Souter); 33tr(Christine Pemberton); 36tr(Robert Aberman); 38t(Leslie Woodhead); 39tl(Sarah Murray), m(Robert Francis), b(Tim Motion); 42bl(Robert Aberman); 43bl(Sarah Murray), br(Robert Francis); 44tl(Tim Motion); 45br(Robert Francis); 50bl(Juliet Highet); 62l(Robert Francis); 70m(Jeremy A. Horner).

Images Colour Library:; 11b; 12b; 13bl, br; 14tr; 15no. 2, no. 5; 25br; 29tr; 41; 84t, bl, br.

The Interior Archive: 8tl(Schulenburg); 9tr(Schulenburg); 67tr (Schulenburg).

Don Morley: 90tr, bl; 91bl, tr.

The Stock Market: 14br; 15no. 1(K. Biggs); 30bl; 31br; 32bl; 39tr; 41bl(B. Simmons); 42t; 44r; 53tr; 55tr; 67r; 77br; 79br(Jon Feingersh); 86m; 85bl; 88br. Tony Stone: 63br (Laurence Monneret); 65tr(Tim Flach); 69br(Robert Mort); 77r(Bruce Ayres); 79tr(Tim Flach); 86tr(Jon Gray); 85tr(Dan Bosler); 88tr(Peter Correz), bl(David Hanover); 89t(Christopher Bissell).

Jessica Strang: 50br; 51tl, bl; 52r; 55l; 58br; 66tl, tr, br; 71l; 73tr, bl, br; 87br.

Superstock: 22tr, m; 23br.

View: 9m(Phillip Bier); 15no. 1(Dennis Gilbert); 30m; 31bl, tl; 32t(Chris Gascoigne), r(Chris Gascoigne); 34-5(Peter Cook); 36b(Dennis Gilbert); 37tr(Peter Cook), br(Chris Gascoigne); 38b(Dennis Gilbert); 40t, b(Peter Cook); 41tr(Chris Gascoigne); 45m(Dennis Gilbert), bl(Dennis Gilbert); 48bl(Chris Gascoigne); 49tr(Peter Cook); 50tr(Dennis Gilbert); 52br(Chris Gascoigne); 53r(Peter Cook), br(Peter Romaniuk); 54tr(Chris Gascoigne), tl(Peter Cook), b(Dennis Gilbert);

56tl(Chris Gascoigne), bl(Peter Cook), br(Dennis Gilbert); 57tl(Dennis Gilbert), l(Chris Gascoigne), bl(Chris Gascoigne), tr(Chris Gascoigne); 58tl(Nick Hufton), tr(Peter Cook); 59r(Chris Gascoigne), bl(Chris Gascoigne); 60tr(Chris Gascoigne), br(Chris Gascoigne); 61bl(Nick Hufton), tr(Chris Gascoigne); 62tr(Chris Gascoigne), bl(Dennis Gilbert), br(Peter Cook); 63t(Nick Hufton), l(Chris Gascoigne); 64t(Nick Hufton), bl(Nick Hufton), br(Peter Cook); 65r(Chris Gascoigne), bl(Peter Cook); 66tl(Chris Gascoigne); 67b(Peter Cook); 68t(Nick Hufton), bl(Peter Cook), br(Chris Gascoigne); 69tr(Chris Gascoigne); 70t(Chris Gascoigne); 71tl(Chris Gascoigne); 72tl(Dennis Gilbert), m(Chris Gascoigne), br(Chris Gascoigne); 73l(Chris Gascoigne); 74-5; 76tl(Chris Gascoigne), br(Chris Gascoigne); 77tl(Peter Cook), bl(Chris Gascoigne); 78t(Peter Cook), b(Dennis Gilbert); 86bl(Chris Gascoigne); 89m(Peter Cook), b(Peter Cook);

Elizabeth Whiting Associates: 30t; 46-7; 51tr; 52tl; 221t; 60bl, b; 70bl, br; 71b.

AUTHOR'S ACKNOWLEDGEMENTS

I should like to thank the staff at Anness Publishing Ltd: Helen Sudell for commissioning the book and Joanne Rippin for managing the project with courage and fortitude, despite the author, and Isobel for keeping her sane.

My family, as ever, deserve praise for their support and tolerance and the anonymous arm with the coffee mug at the end of it deserves a particular mention. Thanks to Tony Holdsworth and Jan Cisek for advice, and to all my friends for keeping off the telephone. A big thank you to Arto for being there and maintaining incredible patience – for a Fire Ox.

BIBLIOGRAPHY

FENG SHUI (GENERAL)

Lau, Theodora, *The Handbook of Chinese Horoscopes* (HarperCollins, London, 1979)

Man-Ho Kwok, Palmer, Martin & Ramsay, Jay, *The Tao Te Ching* (Element, London, 1997)

Ni, Hua-Ching, *The Book of Changes and the Unchanging Truth* (Seven Star Communications, Santa Monica, 1983)

Palmer, Martin, *The Elements of Taoism* (Element, Shaftesbury, 1991)

Palmer, Martin, *Yin and Yang* (Piatkus, London, 1997)

Walters, Derek, *Chinese Astrology* (Aquarian Press, London, 1992)

Walters, Derek, *The Feng Shui Handbook* (Aquarian Press, London, 1991)

Wong, Eva, *Feng Shui* (Shambhala, Boston, 1996)

UNDERSTANDING FENG SHUI

Franz, Marie-Louise von, *Time* (Thames and Hudson, London, 1978)

Jung, Carl, *Man and his Symbols* (Arkana, London, 1990)

Lawlor, Robert, *Sacred Geometry: Philosophy and Practice* (Thames and Hudson, London, 1982)

Lindqvist, Cecilia, *China: Empire of Living Symbols* (Massachusetts, Reading, 1991)

Mann, A.T., *Sacred Architecture* (Element, Shaftesbury, 1993)

Pennick, Nigel, *Earth Harmony: Places of Power, Holiness and Healing* (Capall Bann, Chieveley, 1997)

Poynder, Michael, *Pi in the Sky* (The Collins Press, Cork, 1997)

MODERN FENG SHUI

Cowan, David & Girdlestone, Rodney, *Safe as houses? Ill Health and Electro-Stress in the Home* (Gateway Books, Bath, 1996)

Myers, Norman (ed), *The Gaia Atlas of Planetary Management* (Gaia Book Ltd., London, 1994)

Thurnell-Read, Jane, *Geopathic Stress* (Element, Shaftesbury, 1995)

KI ASTROLOGY

Sandifer, Jon, *Feng Shui Astrology* (Piatkus, London, 1997)

Yoshikawa, *Takashi The Ki* (Rider, London, 1998)

SPACE CLEARING

Kingston, Karen, *Creating Sacred Space with Feng Shui* (Piatkus, London, 1996)

Linn, Denise, *Sacred Space* (Rider, London, 1995)

Treacy, Declan, *Clear your Desk* (Century Business, 1992)

USEFUL ADDRESSES

UK

Gill Hale, M.Ed., Dip.ScGD., RCFSS Consultant for home, office and garden. Workshops, training.
Tel/fax: 020 8688 8516
E-mail: gillhale@mistral.co.uk

THE FENG SHUI ASSOCIATION
Consultations for home, office, garden, signboard and logo design, interior and garden design and building services, clearing intangible forces.
31 Woburn Place, Brighton BN1 9GA
Tel/fax: 01273 693844
E-mail: fengshui@mistral.co.uk
Internet Home Page:
http://www.mistral.co.uk/fengshui

THE FENG SHUI SOCIETY
The Society is an organization representing all the different approaches to Feng Shui, and serves as a focus for the exchange of information.
277 Edgware Road, London W2 1BT
E-mail Karen@fengshuisociety.org.uk

AUSTRALIA

THE FENG SHUI DESIGN STUDIO
PO Box 705, Glebe NSW 2037
612 315 8258

FENG SHUI SOCIETY OF AUSTRALIA
PO Box 1566, Rozelle NSW 2039
612 98101110

FENG SHUI INNOVATIONS
696 Darling Street, Rozelle NSW 2039
612 98101110

FENG SHUI ADVISORY CENTRE
Mosman NSW 2088
612 9751 1016

AUSTRALIAN SCHOOL OF ADVANCED CLASSICAL FENG SHUI
Double Bay NSW 2028
612 9362 8089

FENG SHUI CONSULTANTS
1 Napier Court,
Frankston VIC 3199
613 9776 5439

LIVING CHANGES FENG SHUI & GEOMANCY CONSULTANCY
1 North Court,
Surrey Hills VIC 3127
613 9830 2009

FENG SHUI CONSCIOUS ENVIRONMENT
9 Lima Grove, Northcote VIC 3070
613 9481 1129

USA

AMERICAN FENG SHUI INSTITUTE
108 North Ynez, Suite 202,
Monterey Park CA91754
626 571 2757

FENG SHUI INSTITUTE OF AMERICA
PO Box 488, Wabasso, FL 32970

THE FENG SHUI DIRECTORY AND MAGAZINE
PO Box 6701, Charlottesville, VA 22906
804 974 1726

THE FENG SHUI GUILD
PO Box 766
Boulder, CO 80306
303 444 1548

WESTERN SCHOOL OF FENG SHUI
437 South Hwy 101, Suite 752
Solana Beach, CA 92075
619 793 0945

INDEX